Taxes

FOR BUSY PEOPLE

Other Busy People Books

Personal Finance for Busy People
Robert Cooke

Time Management for Busy People
Roberta Roesch

Stress Management for Busy People
Carol Turkington

Taxes

FOR BUSY PEOPLE

The Book to Use When There's No Time to Lose!

Robert A. Cooke

McGraw-Hill

New York   San Francisco   Washington, D.C.   Auckland   Bogotá
Caracas   Lisbon   London   Madrid   Mexico City   Milan
Montreal   New Delhi   San Juan   Singapore
Sydney   Tokyo   Toronto

Library of Congress Catalog Card Number: 97-075820

McGraw-Hill

A Division of The **McGraw·Hill** *Companies*

1 2 3 4 5 6 7 8 9 0 DOC/DOC 9 0 2 1 0 9 8 7

ISBN 0-07-012557-0

The sponsoring editor for this book was Susan Barry,
the editing supervisor was Rick Soldin,
the designer was Ted Mader Associates,
and the production supervisor was Clare Stanley.
It was set in Adobe Garamond by Electronic Publishing Services, Inc.

Printed and bound by R. R. Donnelley & Sons Company.

McGraw-Hill books are available at special quantity discounts to use as premiums and sales promotions, or for use in corporate training programs. For more information, please write to the Director of Special Sales, McGraw-Hill, 11 West 19th Street, New York, NY 10011. Or contact your local bookstore.

This publication is designed to provide accurate and authoritative information in regard to the subject matter covered. It is sold with the understanding that the publisher is not engaged in rendering legal, accounting, or other professional service. If legal advice or other expert assistance is required, the services of a competent professional person should be sought.

—from a declaration of principles jointly adopted by a committee of the American Bar Association and a committee of publishers

About the Author

Robert Cooke is a Certified Financial Planner, a CPA, and a nationally syndicated columnist who writes on tax and financial issues for entrepreneurs and small business owners. He is the author of several books on finance and financial planning, including *The McGraw-Hill 36-Hour Course on Finance for Nonfinancial Managers.*

Contents
at a glance

Contents

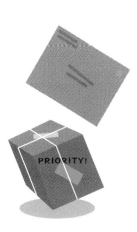

INTRODUCTION

This book is for busy people, people like you who have only a few nights or weekend afternoons to find out everything they need to know about tax payments and deductions, and then sit down and complete those dreaded forms before the ever-approaching April deadline. You don't have time to wade through a backbreaking tax manual to find the necessary information to reduce your taxes. In this book I will help you pinpoint the precise information that you need for your situation, without all the extra tax-babble you *don't* need—hey, you're a busy person; you don't have time for that!

What This Book Will Do for You and How to Use It

You're busy—your life is full of work, family, and other commitments. There is no time left in which you can become a tax expert. There are three directions you can take:

(1) You can take pencil in hand and aspirin in mouth and try to fill in the required forms, perhaps as late as October 14 (the day before the expiration of the final extension). If you want to try to take advantage of every tax break that is available, you might buy a 700-page manual on the federal income tax rules. Then, the question is: When will you find the time to search through 700 pages? Also, not all of the tax rules will fit in 700 pages. (Professional tax manuals may consist of 15 volumes of several hundred pages each.)

(2) You are computer literate and buy one of the software programs that will not only fill in tax forms for you but will do the math and offer some help as to the tax rules. But they can leave you wondering if the program covers all the deductions and tax breaks that are available to you.

(3) You rely on a tax professional not only to prepare your tax return but to give you some guidance as to running your life so that the tax impact is as small as possible. However, if your tax knowledge is very basic, or nonexistent, that guidance and advice are going to cost you, for you will need to spend hours with that professional, describing your business and personal life in much detail and receiving individual tutoring from him or her.

These three methods of tax planning and preparation have one common thread: They don't work well unless you have basic knowledge of the tax rules. That knowledge can help you pick out the few pages of the 700-page manual that apply to you. It can make you aware when you need more help and explanation than the software help-screens provide, and it can help you organize your tax life so that the expensive time spent with a professional is short.

And there are more timesavers in this book. At the beginning of each chapter is a list of who should read that chapter, as well as a list of what is included in the chapter. You need read only what applies to you.

Then, armed with your new tax knowledge, you can take one of the three actions listed above. Frankly, I recommend number three (use a professional). A good tax advisor will usually save you far more than his or her fee. How do you find a good one? That's in Chapter 12 of this book.

Things You Might
Want to Know About This Book

You can read this book more or less in any order. Use the book as a reference. When you're stuck—not sure how to do something—and you know there must be an answer, just pick up the book, zero in on the solution to your problem and put the book down again. Besides the clear, coherent explanations of tax rules, the book includes some special elements to help you hold on to more of your hard-earned cash as you navigate through the task of tax preparation. Here's a quick rundown:

Fast Forward

Every chapter begins with a section called *Fast Forward*. Each of these sections is, in effect, a book within a book—a built-in quick reference guide, summarizing the key tasks explained in the chapter that follows. If you're a fast learner, or somewhat experienced, the Fast Forwards may be the only material you need. Written step-by-step, point-by-point, they even include page references to guide you to the more complete information later in the chapter.

Expert Advice

Timesaving tips, techniques, and worthwhile addictions are all reported under the rubric of *Expert Advice*. (Look for the pensive scientist.) Force yourself to develop some good habits now, while it's still possible! These notes also give you the big picture and help you plan ahead.

Caution

Sometimes it's too easy to plunge ahead and fall down a manhole, resulting in hours of extra work just to get you back to where you were before you went astray. This icon will warn you before you commit time-consuming mistakes.

Definition

If you encounter words you don't recognize, look for this bodybuilder in the margin. *Definitions* point out important terms that you might not reasonably know the meaning of. When necessary, definitions are strict and a little technical, but most of the time they're informal and conversational.

New Law Toll Booths

Look for *New Law Toll Booths* in the margin to alert you to recent changes in the tax laws for the coming year.

Throughout the book, cross-references and other minor asides appear in margin notes like this one.

Let's Do It!

Income Tax on What Your Employer Pays You

WHO SHOULD READ THIS CHAPTER

- Everyone who has a job or is looking for a job
- Everyone who is self-employed in his or her own business. (If you are self-employed, you might save taxes by setting up your business as a corporation and paying yourself. You then become your own employee. More about this is in Chapter 5.)

THIS CHAPTER INCLUDES

- Cash you receive for your work—what's taxable and what isn't
- Other compensation (benefits) you receive for your work—what's taxable and what isn't, including:

Meals and lodging	Life insurance
Employee discounts	Adoption assistance
Achievement awards	Day-care benefits
Health and accident plans	

- Deciphering your W-2—where the numbers come from

FAST FORWARD

Cash Compensation ➤ pp. 4–5

Generally, cash wages and salaries are all taxable. But not all cash received from your employer is wages and salaries; it could be reimbursement of expenses. ("Cash" includes payment by check or electronic deposit.)

Noncash Compensation ➤ pp. 5–12

There are several payments your employer can make to you or for you that may not incur tax. **Important**: Your employer has to pay for the following items for you. You cannot get a tax deduction by buying these items yourself.

- Lodging and food. Do you have to live at your work site for the convenience of your employer?
- Health and accident plans. Usually, medical insurance, membership in a health maintenance organization, and money invested in a medical savings account escape income tax.
- Life insurance. If the plan is structured correctly, you can receive some of this benefit tax-free or with a relatively small tax bite.

Big Brother (your friendly IRS) has made tax paying painless (?) to you and tax collecting easy for it. For about 60 years we have suffered the pay-as-you-go withholding system, under which you never see all the money for which you work so hard. The government forces your employer to divert much of your money out of your paycheck before it arrives in your hands or bank account. The result: Many people are duped. They forget about the taxes withheld and think they are well off tax-wise if, early in the next year, they receive a refund of excess withholding. Don't be taken in by this scheme. Look at your Form W-2. Add the income tax withheld to twice the Social Security tax withheld. Couldn't you spend most of that 30 to 50 percent of your earnings more wisely than do the Congress, the president, and the bureaucrats? In other words, reducing the tax that's the bottom line on your tax form will increase your refund, and that's more of your money coming back to you.

Besides cash, there are several other ways in which an employer can compensate an employee for his or her services. Usually, they are called "fringe benefits," and some of these noncash payments are just as taxable as cash. (Example: Expense-paid trip to take the family to Disney World.) Other fringe benefits are not taxable, or at least not taxable until sometime in the future.

If you work for a large organization, the executive suite and the stable of lawyers, accountants, and consultants probably ensure that the numbers on your W-2 reflect what is taxable and omit what isn't taxable. However, if you work for a small shop, your employer may not be aware of how he or she can channel tax-free benefits to you and other employees. Both you and your employer can benefit from tax-free or tax-delayed benefits.

Example: You receive a tax-free benefit of $100. You have the equivalent of $100 more in your pocket, and that $100 has cost your employer only $100. On the other hand, if your employer wants to put $100 cash in your pocket, what he or she will have to pay you looks like this:

Gross pay	$155.40	
Subtract:		
Income tax (28% bracket)	$ 43.51	
Social Security tax	11.89	
Total subtractions		55.40
Net pay		$100.00

But that is not all it costs your employer. The company must also match the Social Security tax that is withheld from your pay. So the employer's cost is even higher.

Gross pay	$155.40
Employer's share of Social Security tax	11.89
Total cost to employer	$167.29

So, it costs your employer $167.29 for you to receive $100. No wonder non-taxable fringe benefits are popular.

Cash Compensation—What Is Taxed?

Not everything that flows from your employer to you is necessarily compensation for your hard work. Some of that flow from your employer may be reimbursement of expenses. If properly handled, that does not count as income to you. For instance, you stop by the office supply store and spend $30 of your money for a box of copy paper for your boss. The following day the company gives you a check for $30.

That's not taxable income to you. It's simply a reimbursement of money you advanced for the company. In Chapter 2 there is more about how these expense reimbursements should be handled.

Meals and Lodging

Meals that are provided by your employer are not taxable income to you if:

- The meals are provided on the employer's premises.
- They are provided for the convenience of the employer.

DEFINITION

"Convenience of the employer" means that your not leaving the premises during a meal benefits the employer. Example: A hospital requires emergency room personnel to eat on the premises at no charge so they will be immediately available if needed.

Lodging provided by your employer is not taxable income to you if:

- The lodging is provided on the employer's premises.
- It is provided for the convenience of the employer.
- You must occupy the quarters as a condition of employment.

DEFINITION

"Condition of employment" means that your employer requires you to be on the premises. Examples: Managers of hotels or self-storage operations.

Example: If Joan, your employer, lends you a new travel trailer, that you can park anywhere and live in or not live in, the rental value of that travel trailer is taxable income to you. (That value should be included in your W-2.) However, if she parks her travel trailer at her construction site, hires you as her superintendent, and insists that you live in the travel trailer, the rental value of the travel trailer should not be taxable.

What if she gives you a cash allowance so that you can rent the apartment across the street from her construction site? The IRS says that a cash allowance is income and must be included in the total income shown on your W-2. This does not mean you can deduct the apartment or trailer rent from your income. You will end up paying tax on that cash allowance. (You might be able to claim a deduction for rent if the job is temporary, but that's tough to prove and claiming it might invite an IRS audit.)

Where on the tax forms do you deduct these nontaxable items from your income? You don't, because they should not show up on your W-2 in the first place.

EXPERT ADVICE

If you are required to live and/or eat at your job, make sure your employer provides these quarters and meals to you. Do not accept a cash allowance.

Health and Accident Plans

Although your employer had an arduous task in satisfying the IRS requirements when the company set up a medical plan, there is little required of you except to make sure claims for reimbursement for medical expenses are filed with the plan. Although any medical plan is valuable, that value never shows up in your W-2 nor is it otherwise taxable this year or in any year. (That assumes that the plan does meet the IRS requirements.)

Common types of medical plans are the following.

Medical Insurance

The employer buys medical insurance for you, so you look to the insurance company to pay for your illnesses and accidents. (Large employers may self-insure a medical plan. That is, the company, rather than an insurance company, may pay your medical bills, but it makes little difference to an employee.)

Heath Maintenance Organizations (HMOs)

Where these popular organizations are used, the employer pays an HMO to "manage" your medical care by requiring that you use only the doctors, hospitals, and pharmacies with whom they have contracts.

Medical Savings Account (MSA)

This is your account into which your small employer can make contributions, up to a specified amount, that are considered nontaxable income to you. You may use the funds only to pay medical expenses in this year or future years. The plan is specifically designed to pay the deductible part of a high-deductible medical insurance policy.

For MSA purposes, a "small employer" is defined as one who employs no more than 50 employees.

Life Insurance

Your employer may provide a group term-life insurance program for employees. Premiums for a death benefit of up to $50,000 are not income to you, and for greater benefit amounts, the tax bite may be small. (The small size of the tax bite is due to the insurance cost tables the IRS uses.) If some of the cost of this life insurance is taxable to you, your employer should include it in the taxable income box of your W-2.

Cafeteria Plans

This is part of the tax law that lets you pick and choose. If your employer offers one of these plans, it means that you can choose benefits for yourself from a menu of several benefits. The menu can include:

- Group term-life insurance
- Accident and health plan
- Dependent care assistance
- Vacation days—provided they do not carry over to future years and you cannot receive cash in lieu of the vacation

Other Fringe Benefits

The IRS gives you no more breaks than it has to. Accordingly, it views fringe benefits this way: The values of all fringe benefits are taxable unless the benefits are specified as nontaxable by the tax law. The most common nontaxable fringe benefits, in addition to those we have discussed, are these:

No Additional Cost Service

If the service that your employer provides to you generates no additional expense to the employer, the value of that service is not taxable.

Example: You work for the Flapping Wing Airline. The plane to Toledo has 300 seats, but only 250 have been sold. You want to go to Toledo to visit your grandmother, so you slide into seat number 251 and go at no charge. Because the plane (and your seat) is going to Toledo, anyway, whether or not *you* go, there is no additional cost to your employer, so the value of the flight is not taxable to you.

For this to work, your employer's policy in this area cannot discriminate in favor of top management.

Qualified Employee Discount

This is the situation in which you as an employee are eligible to buy the product or service of your employer at a discount. If the discount meets certain rules, your employer does not have to treat the discount as additional wages paid to you.

Example: You work for the Nosole Shoe Store. The store's employee policy is that you can buy shoes, for your own use only, at the store's cost. The **papier-mâché** shoes you buy normally sell for $100 a pair, but you buy them at cost—$55. In theory, you have saved $45 because you work at the store, so the $45 is in the nature of payment to you. However, so long as you are not charged less than the store's cost, the tax law says that's okay—you pay no income tax on the $45 savings.

Example: You work for the Gooey Carpet Cleaning Company. Last Tuesday you hired your employer to clean the carpet in your home. The normal charge for your size of carpet is $100. If you pay your employer at least $80, the tax law again says that's okay—no income tax involved.

THE RULE IS

To avoid your employee discount being taxed as income, you must pay at least the cost of a product, or at least 80 percent of the usual price of a service.

Working Condition Fringe Benefits

This is a somewhat oblique term that essentially refers to payments your employer makes to you that cover deductible business expenses. For instance, assume you are a securities analyst, working for the Watered Stock Brokerage Firm. You subscribe to *The Wall Street Journal* at a cost of $180. Because it's business-related, you could deduct that $180 as an employee of Watered Stock. However, your employer reimburses you the $180. That money is not income to you because the deduction would offset it. (But see Chapter 4 for more discussion of employee expenses and why employer reimbursement saves taxes.)

Qualified Transportation Fringe

Your employer can pay some of your commuting expenses for you as a nontaxable fringe benefit. The expenses that qualify are these:

1. Commuting transportation in a "commuter highway vehicle." The tax code describes that conveyance as one that can carry six or more passengers plus the driver and that has at least half of the passenger seats occupied. Also, the vehicle must be used at least 80 percent for commuting.
2. Passes or tokens for rail, bus, or ferry mass transit.

   Numbers 1 and 2, together, are limited to $65 per month.
3. Parking, either near the employer's shop or where you catch the mass transit.

   Number 3 is limited to $65 per month.

De Minimis Fringes

The tax law and the IRS actually recognize that some fringe benefits are so small that the accounting to keep track of them would be very burdensome. (As if the whole tax code isn't burdensome!) Examples are occasional supper money and other meals, taxi fare after overtime work, occasional use of the copy machine, occasional employee parties, and small gifts.

Meals at Employer-operated Facilities

If you buy lunch (or any meal) at an eating facility provided by your employer, you probably pay much less than you would down the street at a commercial restaurant. The saving is money in your pocket, but it's not taxable to you so long as the price covers the cost of the food and the labor involved. (The price does not need to cover the cost of space, equipment depreciation, and other overhead.)

Employee Achievement Awards

You pay no tax on these, as long as they are tangible awards and the value does not exceed $400. (In certain instances, the award may be as much as $1,600, but it has to be made as part of a formal plan by your employer.)

Employer-provided Adoption Assistance

Tax benefit extended

Your employer may pay you (or foot the bills) for your adoption of a child, up to a limit of $5,000 ($6,000 for a special-needs child) without the benefit being taxable to you. The maximum benefit is phased down if your income is over $75,000, and the benefit disappears at an income level of $115,000.

Educational Assistance Programs Provided by an Employer

Your employer can spend up to $5,250 for your education without your having to pay tax on that benefit. The education can be in any subject or field, but it cannot be at the graduate level. (Graduate-level education was included for only the first six months of 1996.)

Congress has a history of letting this nontaxable benefit expire and resurrecting it later. At one point, the revival came so late that many people paid taxes on the educational assistance they received even though it later turned out it was not taxable.

If you received educational assistance from your employer in 1995 and 1996 and paid income tax on the value of the assistance, you may be due a refund of income tax from the IRS, as well as a refund from your employer of the Social Security tax on the benefit. If you have not received help from your employer in obtaining these refunds, ask for the help. (The IRS issued guidelines to employers on August 23, 1996, in a document called the *Income Tax Information Release No. 96-36 of August 23, 1996.*)

EXPERT ADVICE

This benefit is for all undergraduate study. If you take courses that are related to your job (but not to a new job), your employer can reimburse you for the cost without any limit in the amount, and graduate level courses could qualify.

Tuition Reduction Programs

If you are employed by an educational institution, you and members of your family are probably eligible for reduced tuition. If you use this benefit, the amount of the tuition reduction (i.e., discount) is not taxable to you.

Dependent Care Benefits

Your employer can pay your dependent care expenses to you, tax-free, up to $5,000. This does, however, reduce the credit you can take for child-care expenses. (See Chapter 2.)

Valuation of Taxable Fringe Benefits

Although many fringe benefits that your employer can provide generate no additional income tax for you to pay, other benefits have no such advantage. Yet, compensation packages, particularly for executives, often include benefits that are not tax-free. If you receive such a benefit, the value of them must be included in your income.

(Your employer should include that value in your W-2, but if it's not there, you are supposed to report that value as wages and salaries.)

What is the value of a taxable fringe benefit? For items such as country club membership, it's the total of the dues and other fees that your employer pays. That's easy to compute. However, some taxable fringe benefits consist of the use of your employer's equipment. Here is how the IRS says this use of facilities should be valued:

Employer-owned Automobiles

If your employer provides you with an automobile for commuting and other personal use, the company should compute the value from the appropriate IRS automobile lease value tables and include that in your W-2.

If you use your employer-provided automobile mainly for business but also use it personally, the value of your personal use can be computed by a cents-per-mile method, using the standard mileage rate as for business use of a personal car.

Employer-provided Flights

The value of these, if they are provided to you for your personal pleasure, is computed by more IRS formulas and instructions. If the flight is commercial, the formulas are based on regular or "space-available" fares. If the flight is on a noncommercial aircraft, it's based on the type of aircraft. The best formula is a "seating capacity" rule: If half of the seats on a noncommercial flight are occupied by other employees on business and you tag along for pleasure, the increase in your taxable income for the fringe benefit is zero.

Transportation Provided Because of Unsafe Conditions

Suppose you have no automobile. To get to and from your night shift work you have to walk through a neighborhood infested with crack houses and drug dealers. The law says that if you commute through unsafe conditions, your employer can provide transportation (or reimburse you for cab fare). That will increase your taxable income only $1.50 for each way of your commute, even though your employer may spend much more.

Sorting Out the Numbers on Your W-2

There are 26 boxes on the 1996 W-2 Form. It's a little overwhelming to find that several boxes are filled in on your W-2. You thought that all you had to worry about was total wages and the income tax withheld. Despite all the other numbers, those two items may be all you need to know, but, just in case, here is a rundown on what the numbers and other information mean:

a. The control number is probably meaningless to you. Some payroll systems use it to keep track of batches or for other internal information.

b. Employer's identification number has little relevance to an employee, unless it has changed from last year. If you think you work for the same employer as last year but this number changes, ask questions. You may have been transferred to another company, and that raises questions about your retirement plan and other benefits.

c. Employer's name and address are obvious.

d. Employee's Social Security number. This should be your number, and make sure that it is. A wrong number can bring you a large pile of correspondence from the IRS and, if not corrected, rob you of some Social Security benefits later in life. Incidentally, this is the number that the IRS uses for its matching program. The Big Brother computer uses your Social Security number to match the copy of your W-2 it receives from your employer to your tax return. If it doesn't find that income on your tax return, you could be in deep trouble.

e. Your name and address.

1. This should include all payments that are taxable to you. Among them are the following:
    *   Wage or salary *paid* (regardless of when earned) during the year.
    *   Tips that you have reported to your employer or that your employer is required to assume you received.

- Taxable reimbursement of expenses, such as travel, entertainment, and moving, even though you may have offsetting deductions. (See Chapter 2.)
- Taxable portion of fringe benefits. (Covered already in this chapter.)
- Other. Your employer should be able to provide a list of the items that are in Box 1.

2. Federal income tax withheld during the year. Remember, this is your money that the government grabs before you see it.

3. For many people, this is the same number as that in Box 1. However, some benefits are subject to Social Security tax but not income tax, so there may be a difference between the amounts in Boxes 1 and 3. Again, your employer should be able to provide you with a breakdown of this figure. In any event, this box should never contain a number greater than the Social Security limit for the year ($65,400 for 1997).

4. This should be 6.2 percent of the figure in Box 3. (It should not be more than $3,887.40 on a 1997 W-2.)

5. Medicare wages and tips. This is computed in the same manner as Box 3, Social Security wages, except that there is no limit.

6. Medicare tax withheld. This is 1.45 percent of Box 5. (Note that if your wages were $1,000,000, your Social Security tax would be the maximum of $3,887.40. However, your Medicare tax would be 1.45 percent of the entire $1,000,000, which is $14,500.)

7. Tips. If you work in a job for which you would be expected to receive tips, you are supposed to report the total tips received to your employer. That figure goes in this box and in Box 1. However, the total of Boxes 3 and 7 should not be more than the Social Security limit ($65,400 in 1997).

8. Allocated tips. This may apply to you if you receive tips as an employee of a food and beverage institution. The IRS expects tips of all tipped employees to be at least 8 percent of sales. If they aren't, your employer may have to "allocate" an assumed tip amount to each employee, so that the total of actual and assumed tips equals the magic 8 percent figure. This can create real problems for you. You have to add this "allocated tip" number to your income in Box 1 and pay tax on it. In addition, you're supposed to pay Social Security taxes (and penalties) on this fictional money.

Avoid this unhappy event! If you keep accurate daily records of the tips you receive, you can ignore this figure in Box 8, even if your total tips are less than 8 percent of the food and beverage you served. The best bet is to use the form the IRS provides for these records (Form 4070A). You also have to report the monthly totals to your employer on Form 4070.

9. Earned income credit payments. If you have earned income of less than a specific amount ($29,290 in 1997), you may be eligible for this credit. If you are eligible, you could ask your employer to pay you the amount of the credit monthly. The total of these monthly payments should be in this box.

10. Dependent care benefits. This is the total amount of child or dependent care benefit you received from your employer. Any amount over $5,000 is taxable and that excess amount will therefore be included in boxes 1, 3, and 5.

11. Nonqualified plans. Some nonqualified plans (usually set up for upper management) generate taxable income in some plan years. When they do, the amount appears in this box and also in Boxes 1, 3, and 5.

12. Benefits included in Box 1. This figure is the total of taxable benefits that are not displayed in Box 10 (dependent care) or Box 13 (described next).

13. See instructions for Form W-2. Here is where the IRS ran out of room on the W-2 Form. They needed 23 other boxes, but the items involved are somewhat uncommon, so the IRS form designers used one box and specified a code to explain the number in the box. The codes are on the back of the employee's copy of the W-2. They are more or less self-explanatory if you have a translation for certain words and numbers. Here is some help:

   - Section 457 plan. This is about deferred compensation (retirement) plans of state/local governments and tax-exempt nonprofit organizations.

   - Uncollected Social Security tax on tips. This arises if you reported tips to your employer but did not provide him or her with the cash to pay your part of the Social Security tax on the tips.

   - Section 401(k). This refers to the plans that let you decide whether you want to put money in a tax-deferred retirement plan or take the taxable cash. (See the earlier discussion in this chapter.)

- Section 403(b). This covers annuities provided, as an employer, by charitable organizations and schools.
- Section 408(k)(6) salary reduction SEP (Simplified Employer Pension Plan). Essentially, this is a cash or deferred plan for small employers.
- Section 501(c)18(D). This refers to employee trusts established before June 25, 1959.

2

Retirement and More Benefits

WHO SHOULD READ THIS CHAPTER

- Everyone who works for a company with these benefits

- Everyone looking for a job with these benefits

- Everyone who is an employer

THIS CHAPTER INCLUDES

- Retirement Plans: Tax-free (deferred, really) money you and your employer can put away for you—background to help you understand the plans your employer may offer

- Stock options (more deferred taxes)

- Nonqualified retirement plans that nevertheless can defer the tax bite

FAST FORWARD

Retirement and Employer-sponsored Savings Plans ➤ pp. 19–25

These plans are great opportunities to invest money before the IRS takes it away from you. True, you eventually pay some income tax on it, but that is after you retire and are probably in a low tax bracket.

Employer's Stock and Stock-option Plans ➤ pp. 25–27

Here's a method your employer can use to get you to work a little harder or smarter. If the company's stock price goes up, you make some money without having to invest anything out of your pocket. You pay no tax until you have your gains in hand.

Nonqualified Benefit Plans ➤ p. 28

If you are in the executive ranks, this is a way your employer can set aside more retirement funds for you than are set aside for other employees. The downside: more risk, more dependency on the continuing solvency of your employer.

Retirement and Savings Plans (Set Up and Run by Your Employer)

These are plans which, if properly designed and approved by the IRS, allow your employer to shelter some of your income. Example: Your employer budgets $50,000 per year for your compensation. He or she could pay you the full $50,000, leaving you to pay the income tax and Social Security tax on that amount. Or your employer could pay you only $45,000 in cash and put the other $5,000 in a retirement plan for you. Now you pay income and Social Security taxes on only the $45,000. That means the whole $5,000 goes to work, earning interest or dividends while it is in your retirement plan. Your employer does get to deduct the $5,000 from the company's income, so in effect the government gets no income tax from the plan until you retire, and it never collects any Social Security tax on the money that goes into the plan.

Types of Retirement Plans and Choices You Can Make

Don't try to become a retirement plan expert. There are over 200 IRS regulations covering this area, many of them are lengthy, and all are complex. It is enough that you understand at least the basic concepts of your employer's plan. The following basic descriptions of the types of plans may help you fathom the plan you're in and what, if any, tax-saving actions you can take.

Pension Plan (the Old Classic)

This is technically called a "Defined Benefit Plan," for your monthly pension can be fairly accurately determined several years before you retire. Your pension will be based on a formula that involves your earnings during your employment and your length of service. Your employer is supposed to dump enough money into the plan every year to make sure that the funds will be there to pay pensions to you and your fellow retirees. No action is required on your part, except to take care of yourself so that you will live to enjoy the pension. (Your pension will be taxable. See Chapter 9 for taxes you will pay on the benefits.)

Profit-sharing Plans

The technical term here is "Defined Contribution Plan." Here, your employer dumps a specific amount of money (the defined contribution) into the plan every year. The plan trustee invests the money, and how much retirement money you will receive will depend on how well the investments do. In some plans, you are allowed to direct the plan trustee as to the investments you want your funds in. Again, you pay no tax now on what your employer contributes, for you, to the plan. (The "profit-sharing" is something of misnomer. The contributions can be made regardless of what the employer's profits are. Usually, the contributions are a percentage of your compensation.)

Stock-bonus Plans

The technical name here is "Employee Stock Ownership Plan" (ESOP). Basically, it is a profit-sharing (defined contribution) plan that is invested in your employer's stock. These plans at some point will give you the option of diversifying by selling your employer's stock and replacing it with other investments, *within* the plan. As long as you don't take the investments or cash out of a defined-contribution plan, there are no tax consequences to selling and buying investments in the plan.

Cash-or-Deferred Plans—Also Known as Section 401(k) Plans

This is an embellishment of profit-sharing or defined contribution plans. In these, as part of the company's budget for your services, is included a contribution to a defined contribution plan. But if you act before the end of the year, you can tell your employer to pay you in cash instead of making a contribution to the plan.

Your decision can have a significant effect on the taxes you pay. If you direct your employer to make a contribution to your retirement, rather than cash, that contribution is not taxable to you now. It does not show up in taxable wages on your W-2. (Again, see Chapter 9 for the taxes you may pay when you retire.) However, if you insist on cash, that is immediately taxable to you.

Example: You are paid $40,000 per year, plus you are eligible for a $4,000 contribution to a retirement plan. If you so specify, before a specific date (of which your employer should notify you), you can receive the $4,000 in cash.

What does this do to your tax bill? Assume you are in the lowest tax bracket of 15 percent. That extra $4,000 you take in cash raises your income tax bill by $600, and it raises your Social Security tax by $280. You will pay $880 in order to get your hands on the extra $4,000! If your employer matches part of your contribution, the $4,000 cash costs you even more (the amount of the contribution your employer did not make because you didn't elect to have the $4,000 contribution made for you). Suggestion: If you need the money, try to get it some other way.

Annuities

If you work for a nonprofit organization, your retirement plan may consist of an annuity, usually sold and managed by an insurance company. In simple terms, your employer makes payments to an insurance company on your behalf; the insurance company sticks the payments into various investments. In return, when you retire, the insurance company will pay you a certain amount every month for as long as you live. (In some plans, the payments continue until both you and your spouse have died.) The immediate tax effect of an annuity plan is that the payments your employer makes to the insurance company on your behalf are not taxable income to you. (Again, see Chapter 9 as to taxability of benefits.)

What You Need to Do About Your Retirement Plan and Taxes

Increase Your Fun-later Fund

Take whatever action your plan allows that will increase your employer's contributions to your retirement. This not only reduces your taxes this year but lets the money in the plan earn interest, dividends, and capital gains with no tax to pay until years later (when you retire).

Read Your Employer's Description of Your Retirement Plan

If there is anything you do not understand, ask your employer for an explanation.

Read the Annual Statements

You should receive at least an annual statement of the balance in your retirement plan, as well as other information. Double-check the numbers, comparing them to last year's report.

Tax Planning Implications

There is not much you can do to change your situation with old-style pension plans. If you are in one of these, you know that your pension will be X dollars at age Y. That kind of plan is technically called a "Defined Benefit Plan."

The other kinds of plans, which go by such various names as 401(k), cash-or-deferred, and retirement savings, fall into the broad category of "Defined Contribution Plans." They often allow you some flexibility in how much money is put away for you and therefore not immediately taxed. For a couple of reasons, the more money you can put into these plans, the better off you will be.

First: In many plans, your employer will match some of what you save in these plans. You put a dollar away toward retirement; your employer will also toss a dollar into the plan. Your money has doubled instantly!

Second: Look at the tax saving. If you have an income of about $60,000, and if $5,000 of that is diverted into a retirement plan, your taxes are reduced by almost $1,300 (for a couple with two children taking the standard deduction).

Individual Retirement Account (IRA)

If your employer does not provide a retirement plan, you can do the same thing by setting up an Individual Retirement Account (IRA) for yourself and your spouse, and the deduction will reduce your taxable income, almost as if your employer had made a retirement plan contribution for you.

But note this difference: In the case of a plan to which your employer makes payments, that money does not show up in the taxable income on your W-2. That means that it is not subject to Social Security taxes. However, if you are accumulating retirement funds through an IRA, you do so with money that is included in your taxable income. You do pay Social Security taxes on the money you receive and then put in your IRA. (You do not pay income tax on that money, however, because the deductible contribution has the effect of lowering the amount of your income that is taxable.)

You and your spouse, together, must have compensation that is equal to the amount you invest in an IRA, up to a $4,000 maximum investment. That $4,000 may have been earned by either spouse, or both. If you are single, the maximum investment is $2,000.

DEFINITION

"Compensation" essentially is the money you receive in exchange for your hard work—that is, wages, salaries, commissions, tips, bonuses, and similar items. It is not interest, rents, dividends, and other unearned income.

Even if your employer does provide a retirement plan, you can still contribute to an IRA if your adjusted gross income is not over $40,000 (married couple) or $25,000 (single) in 1996.

For 1998 and beyond, Congress has raised the limits. For joint returns, the limit on adjusted gross income (AGI) for an IRA deduction is $50,000, and that rises each year until it reaches $80,000 in 2007. For singles, the 1998 figure is $30,000, rising to $50,000 in 2005.

DEFINITION

Adjusted gross income (AGI) is defined in Chapter 11. A short definition is that it is your income minus all deductions that are not itemized deductions.

If your income is higher, you can still make contributions (up to the $2,000/$4,000 annual limit), but they will generate little or no immediate tax deduction for you. The only benefit of making this taxable contribution is that the earnings on the contribution build up in the IRA without immediate tax on them. (The earnings will be taxed when you withdraw them.)

Will those nondeductible contributions create problems for you? Probably, when you retire, for you will then need to know how much of your contributions was deductible and how much was not deductible. See the sections about withdrawing retirement money from various plans in Chapter 9.

That last paragraph is the case for 1997 income. For years after 1997, the new Roth IRA is a better choice if your contributions are not deductible.

Roth IRAs

Roth IRAs

Starting in 1998, you can make contributions to this new form of an IRA. You still must meet the compensation test of $2,000/$4,000, but you are not shut out of this program even if you are covered by an employer plan.

The downside of a Roth IRA is that your contributions are nondeductible. In other words, you will have to earn considerably more than $2,000 in order to make a $2,000 contribution.

The upside is that your contributions sit in your Roth IRA, and the interest, dividends, capital gains, and other earnings accumulate tax-free. When you withdraw the funds, if you follow the rules, you pay no tax on the money withdrawn. In other words, the earnings on your investment in a Roth IRA never are taxed.

There is a high limit on adjusted gross income for making contributions to a Roth IRA, but it is much higher than for a regular IRA. Specifically, an individual's ability to make a contribution is reduced if adjusted gross income is over $95,000 for a year, and he or she can make no contribution if the AGI is over $110,000. For a married couple filing a joint return, those numbers are $150,000 and $160,000.

EXPERT ADVICE

Note that if you earn too much to make a contribution to a Roth IRA, you can still make a contribution to a regular IRA. If you are not a participant in an employer's retirement plan, your deduction will be deductible. If you are covered by an employer's plan, your deduction will not be deductible but the earnings will accrue with no tax until you withdraw them.

The Rules for a Roth IRA

- You can make contributions even after age 70½.
- You cannot receive a distribution from the IRA until five years after making a contribution to the IRA.
- After the five-year period, distributions must be made after age 59½. In the event of death, disability, or for first-time home buyer's expenses, distributions can be made earlier.

Converting a Regular IRA to a Roth IRA

Even though you are not yet 59½, you can roll over funds from a regular IRA to a Roth IRA without any penalty for early withdrawal of the funds. You do have to pay your regular income tax on the amount rolled over, as if it were a distribution, but the advantage would be that the earnings on your investment in the Roth IRA are not taxed.

Tax Records You Should Keep

Except for IRAs, your employer has the record-keeping and reporting burden in this area. Do keep the reports of your retirement funds that the company gives you, and keep them at least until you retire. You will probably never need them, but just in case. . . . (Companies do lose records when they merge, spin off, declare bankruptcy, or just go out of business.)

If you own all or a substantial part of the company you work for, your tax planning opportunities in this area are much greater. See Chapter 5.

This discussion requires use of the terms "ordinary income" and "capital gains." These terms are defined and discussed in Chapter 7.

Employer Stock and Stock-Option Plans

The company that employs you may have various plans that enable you to own some of the company's stock or options on stock. (An option is the right to buy a certain number of shares of the stock, at a specific price, in the future.) These plans fall into the following categories.

Nonqualified Stock Options

If the option you receive today enables you to buy the stock at today's market price, you have received something that has no value until the price of the stock goes up. If you then exercise the option and sell the stock after the price goes up, you will make a profit, and that profit will be taxable income.

Example: When your employer's stock is selling on the stock exchange for $100 a share, the company gives you an option to buy ten shares at $100. (The option has no value, as you can buy any number of shares for $100 each at any brokerage house, with or without the option.) Six months later, the price of the stock on the stock exchange has risen to $120 per share. You can now exercise your option and buy the ten shares at only $100 each, and then immediately sell them at the market price of $120. You have made a profit of $20 per share, or a total of $200, and that profit is taxable income.

Note that this income occurs and becomes taxable when you sell the shares, not when you receive the option. Also, if on the day you receive it, the option allows you to buy the stock for less than the market price, you may have immediate income in the amount of the difference between the market price and the lower price (the exercise price) at which you can buy the stock. (However, see the next section on restricted options.)

Restricted Stock and Stock Options

Even if stock and stock options that your employer gives you appear to have immediate value but your ability to sell the stock or exercise the option is restricted, you do not have immediate taxable income. Restriction could occur because you are not allowed to sell the stock until some future date or some event occurs.

Example: If you are given stock that you cannot sell until you have been employed for five years, the stock is restricted. In the fifth year, the value of the stock becomes income to you. If the stock price was $20 per share when it was given to you and $100 per share in the fifth year, you would have to report ordinary (not capital gain) income of $100 per share in that fifth year.

You do have the option, however, of paying ordinary income tax on the $20 per share value when you receive the stock. Then, when you sell the stock years later at $100 per share, the $80 increase in value would be taxed to you at capital gain rates. (See Chapter 7 for a discussion of capital gains.)

EXPERT ADVICE

If your current income is low and you are therefore in a low tax bracket, consider opting to pay the tax on the value of the stock when you receive it, particularly if you expect to be in a high income bracket when you sell the stock. The computations to determine if that is a wise course are complex, so hire an good accountant to help you.

Stock Appreciation Rights (SARs)

These plans actually generate bonuses rather than stock ownership. If you receive an SAR when your employer's stock is worth $20 a share and exercise the SAR when the stock is selling for $100 a share, you will receive a check from your employer for $80 times the number of SARs you exercise—and that check will be ordinary taxable income.

Tax Records to Keep

Because these are employer-sponsored plans, your employer has the burden of keeping the records and including the income, when it should be taxed, on your W-2. However, keep the paperwork you receive on these plans at least until three years after you report the resulting income—just in case.

Tax Planning Implications

Planning in this area is not so much involved with taxes as it is with the present and future value of your employer's stock. You may want to enlist the help of an investment professional in guessing at future stock prices.

Nonqualified Benefit Plans

If you are an executive of a company, your employer may offer benefit plans for executives only. Because they are not available to rank-and file employees, the IRS classifies them as "discriminatory" and therefore "nonqualified." That means that when you receive these benefits, some or all of their value (which usually equals the cost of the benefit to your employer) may be immediately taxable to you.

That would make it sound as if a nonqualified retirement plan would be of no value, for you would have to include the value of the annual addition to your retirement benefit in your income each year. However, the law provides an escape from that burden.

If your employer only makes a promise to provide you with X number of dollars upon retirement but does not fund it (set the money aside in a trust or similar investment vehicle) and does not give you a promissory note, you do not pay tax on the money until the year in which you receive it. Sometimes there is logic behind the tax rules, and the logic here is that you have some risk of not receiving this money. For instance, if your employer files for bankruptcy, you would be only an unsecured creditor. Your "retirement" money might be zero!

Tax Records to Keep

Your employer has most of the record-keeping burden, insofar as what is taxable while you're working. However, records do become lost in the processes of mergers, divestitures, reorganizations, bankruptcies, fires, and floods, so keep the benefit reports your employer gives you. In particular, keep records of retirement plans and life insurance. They may be important in computing income taxes in your retirement years.

Taking Cash Out of Your Retirement Plan

This chapter has concentrated on handling pension plans during your working years. The retirement benefits are discussed in Chapter 9, which is primarily for those who have already retired. (They don't need to read this chapter.) Although you are still working, take a look at the taxes you might pay on those benefits.

If you find yourself in this list, it does not mean you automatically can withdraw funds from your retirement plan for these purposes. It does mean you should read about withdrawals in Chapter 9.

Also, there are circumstances when you can take some money out of an employer's retirement plan or an IRA before retirement. If you have any of these situations, you should read Chapter 9.

- Total disability for an indefinite period
- Excessive medical expense (over 7.5 percent of your adjusted gross income)
- Unemployed for 12 or more weeks
- Pursuing a higher education (yourself or family members)
- First-time home buyer

CHAPTER

Our Favorite Deductions—
Travel and Entertainment

WHO SHOULD READ THIS CHAPTER

- Those who travel and entertain in the course of their employment or self-employment

- Every employer who hires employees who incur travel and entertainment expenses

THIS CHAPTER INCLUDES

- How to deduct transportation expenses in town

- How to compute the deduction of transportation expenses

- What out-of-town travel expenses are deductible

- How to compute out-of-town travel expenses

- How to take your spouse and deduct the travel expenses of both of you

- How to mix vacation with business trips and deduct most of the cost

- How to deduct all the expenses of a foreign business/vacation trip

FAST FORWARD

Travel Expenses ➤ pp. 34–43

- Commuting to and from work. For most of us, there is no deduction for this. There's some, but very little, exception for those who have heavy tools.

- Local business-related transportation after you get to work. The use of your car, a taxi, a bus, or a trolley can be a tax deduction. It's best to have your employer reimburse you for this rather than take a salary increase to cover it.

- Travel out of town on business (includes your car, or a rental car, a plane, train, ship, or stagecoach, as well as hotels, motels, and B&Bs). These are usually all deductible, but there are special rules if you take along your significant other and he or she has no business reason for accompanying you.

Entertainment Expenses ➤ pp. 43–48

- Meals for yourself while in town. The hot dog you grabbed at the lunch counter is a personal expense and nondeductible, as is a six-course dinner you ate on the way home.

- Meals you buy for yourself on the road out of town. You can deduct only 50 percent of these expenses.

- Meals in or out of town for you and for your guests that qualify as entertainment expense. You can deduct only 50 percent of these expenses.

- Pass the "Directly-Related-to-Your-Business Test" to see if you can legally deduct the cost of entertainment.

Perhaps no other section of the Internal Revenue Code receives more attention than the rules about travel and entertainment. It seems to be the favorite subject of most IRS auditors. The reason is that what is legitimate business travel, lodging, meals, and entertaining is not only open to much argument; it is also difficult to define. Add to that the fact that it is an area open to fraud and attractive to cheaters, and you have a solid reason for this advice:

Know the rules. Know what the law allows. And be prepared for an IRS auditor who presumes you overstepped the bounds of law and overstated your expenses.

The Confusion of Terms and What They Usually Mean

The terminology the IRS and most tax experts use in this area can be confusing, so let's start with some clarification of the terms.

* "Transportation" generally refers to *local* transportation within a metropolitan area. Think of it as any moving about that you do that does not take you so far out of town that you have to stay overnight. This transportation might take place in your own vehicle, your employer's vehicle, a taxi, a trolley, a bus, or a rickshaw.

* "Travel" usually refers to your being out of town overnight. Again, it can be in any type of conveyance.

* "Entertainment" means, according to the IRS, "any activity which is . . . generally considered to constitute entertainment, amusement, or recreation." (Only the IRS can define a word by using the word itself.)

* "T & E" is an abbreviation of "Travel and Entertainment" and includes related transportation. It is often used because it is easier to refer to the complex rules in this area as one composite lump of regulations.

Travel and Transportation

Running (or Driving) Around Town

Personal Errands

You make a trip to the hardware store to buy grass seed for the lawn around your home: That's a personal expense, which means there is no tax deduction here.

Commuting

You travel from home to your office, store, factory, or wherever you work: That's a cost of working, but the IRS says "tough." This is only another personal expense with no tax deduction. Here are some details and exceptions:

Extra Cost of Commuting with Heavy Machinery If you have heavy tools or machinery that require you to tow a trailer while commuting, the cost of the trailer is deductible. (That's probably an insignificant figure unless you are renting a trailer.) The extra cost of having to use a pickup truck or van is not deductible, as it is still your basic transportation.

Commuting to a Temporary Work Location

Temporary Work Outside of Your Metropolitan Area If you commute to a *temporary* work location outside of your metropolitan area, you can deduct the cost. Example: You live and work in Atlanta, but you are assigned to a three-week task in Macon (50 miles away). The commuting would be deductible.

Temporary Work within Your Metropolitan Area If you have a *regular work location (or locations) that is not in your home* and commute to a temporary work location within your metropolitan area, you can also deduct your commuting cost. This rule would shoot down your commuting expense if you work out of your home but have no office area in your home that would meet the IRS requirement for a deductible office-in-home. Suggestion: If you work for one employer but usually work at other in-town locations, insist that you be furnished a desk or work area in your employer's office. Then you would satisfy this rule and be able to deduct the expense of commuting from home to temporary locations.

Temporary Work When You Have No Regular Work Location However, if you do not have a regular work location, you cannot deduct the commuting costs. (This would apply if you sign up with a temporary help agency that sends you to various employers for a few days or weeks at a time.)

CAUTION

What is temporary? The IRS defines it as performing work on an irregular or short-term (a matter of days or weeks) basis. How many weeks? It's not defined. Certainly, though, if your work at the temporary location lasts more than one year, and you deduct the commuting costs, you will have an argument with the IRS. Recommendation: Obtain professional tax help if your temporary assignment drags out for several months.

Commuting Expense If You Make Several Outside Calls During the Day

What if your job requires that you move around town to many locations every day (as would a salesperson or serviceperson)? If you report to your office before starting work and after ending work every day, the rule is cut and dried: Your transportation to your office in the morning and from your office at night is nondeductible commuting expense. However, if you leave home in the morning and go directly to your first call, and return home from the last call of the day, only the transportation from home to the first call and from the last call to home is nondeductible.

If the IRS thinks your records do not accurately reflect proper income and deductions, it has the power to change your numbers so that they "clearly reflect income."

Example: Your office is 50 miles from your home. You leave home in the morning, call on the Curdled Milk Company, which is 10 miles from your home and on the way to the office. After the sales call, you drive on to your office. You have now changed 40 miles of nondeductible commuting expense into deductible business travel expense.

CAUTION

If you normally call on each customer once per month, don't call on the Curdled Milk Company twice a day—on the way to work and on the way home. As it would appear that you are doing this just to increase a tax deduction, the IRS will question this activity and probably disallow much of your business transportation expense, and that will result in a big bill from them. (In addition to the tax you didn't pay, you may also be hit with stiff penalties.)

Transportation Expense When Your Office Is in Your Home

What if your office is in your home? Then your travel is from your breakfast room to your spare bedroom (now an office), and *all* of this local moving about is deductible. *But:* For this to work, your "office in the home" must pass the tests for a legitimate office. (See the discussion of a home office in Chapter 8.)

How to Compute the Cost of Business Transportation

The cost of going by taxi, bus, or camel is obviously what you paid the driver—including tax and tip. If you use your own automobile, you can compute the cost by one of two methods:

- Compute your cost as the IRS rate per mile times the number of miles you traveled for business. (In 1997 this rate was 31.5 cents per mile.) Or,
- You can keep track of all your automobile expenses: gas, oil, repairs, tires, batteries, insurance, taxes, license plates, and depreciation. That's a lot of record keeping, and figuring the depreciation will turn you into an expert depreciation accountant, whether you want to be one or not. Suggestion: If your business mileage is only a few hundred miles per year, use the IRS rate-per-mile method.

Travel Out of Town

What Does and Does Not Count As Travel?

The tax rules define "travel" as essentially travel to the extent that rest is required. If you drive from Norfolk to Richmond (90 miles) attend a meeting, and return home the same day, you are not eligible for *travel* deductions, but you can deduct the *transportation* costs (your car expense). If you stop at a rest stop for a 10-minute rest, that won't count for the "rest" requirement. However, if the meeting lasts into the evening, and you rent a hotel room for a few hours' sleep before heading home, you have "rested" and now fall into the category of out-of-town travel. Why is it to your advantage to fall into the travel-out-of-town category? In addition to expenses for transportation (automobile, taxi, etc.), you can deduct items such as 50 percent of the cost of your meals (including tax and tip) and laundry expenses. Also, of course, you can deduct various expenses that would be classified as business-related anywhere.

CAUTION

In this era of commuter air service, some out-of-town travel can be classified as local transportation—when no extended rest takes place. If you leave your home in Boston in the early morning, fly to New York for a conference, and return to Boston in the late afternoon, the tax rules that apply are those that apply to local transportation.

Here's a checklist of *deductible travel* (significant rest required) expenses:

- Hotel or motel lodging expense
- Meal expenses (50 percent of the cost)
- Telephone, mail, fax, copy charges
- Laundry and cleaning expense
- Business expense that would be deductible if you were in your home town
- Tips and taxes on these expenses (50 percent if on meals)

Travel That Is for Both Business and Pleasure

Your goal in this situation should be to treat as much as possible of this trip as business. How do you do this, in light of the basic rule that, if the primary purpose of the trip is business-related, most of the travel costs are deductible? Here's the rundown.

How to Establish That the Primary Purpose of the Trip Is Business

- Make sure your trip is composed of more business days than personal days, so you can deduct the air fare or other expense of getting to your business/vacation destination. A "business day" is one in which you conduct substantial business.
- For the business days, you can deduct the lodging, meals (50 percent), and the other travel expenses we've already listed. For personal days there is no deduction.
- Stay over Saturday night in order to obtain a cheaper air fare. Even though you spend Saturday "on vacation," it is a business day because your stay has a business reason (to save money on air fare).
- Conduct substantial business on Friday and Monday. That makes Saturday and Sunday into "business days." Now you have four business days. You can still vacation for three days and deduct your travel to and from the location as business.

How much "business" does it take to make a day a business day? Just checking your voice mail won't hack it. You need to spend several hours making calls, holding meetings, or servicing equipment. Err on the side of more time on business—it's safer.

For Foreign Travel, the Rules Are Different

As opposed to domestic travel, deducting the trip to and from a foreign location is an all-or-nothing proposition: the business versus personal expense in foreign travel is allocated. In other words, if four out of 10 days of a business trip to Spain were personal, you would still be able to deduct six-tenths of the cost of the flight to and from Spain, as well as six-tenths of your expenses while there.

In addition, there are some escape hatches from the foreign travel rules. If you pass any of the following, you have a deduction for all the travel expenses of your trip, even though you spent much time sightseeing and windsurfing.

These Can Make Your Foreign Travel 100 Percent Deductible

- If your travel time does not exceed one week, you do not have to allocate expenses. It's all business expense. Of course, the main purpose of the trip has to be business-related. Flying to Scotland to listen to Uncle Angus play the bagpipes is still a personal, nondeductible expense. (To compute one week, do not count the day you leave the United States, but do count the day you return.)

- Keep your sightseeing and other personal time to less than 25 percent of your time abroad, no matter how long that is, and you will be able to deduct all your travel expenses. For this rule, count both the beginning day and the ending day. (Who says the tax rules are consistent?)

- Do you have control over the arranging of the foreign business trip? Unless you are related to your employer, are a managing executive, or own at least 10 percent of your employer, the trip will be considered to be entirely business-related.

- If a personal vacation is not a major reason for making the trip, you can deduct all the travel expenses.

Of course, if the primary reason for the trip is personal, then there is no deduction. If the reason for the trip is business, but vacation is a significant consideration, then the rules for allocation of expense apply.

Allocating Foreign Travel Expenses If you are not eligible for any of the escape hatches just covered, but the trip was primarily for business, you have to allocate expenses of the whole trip between business and pleasure.

To do this, count your "business days." These are days you spent getting there (after you left the United States), any day your presence is required at a particular place for business reasons (even if it is for only a few minutes), any other day you conduct business, and weekends and holidays if they are between business days.

Then add up the total days you spent traveling for both business and pleasure.

Divide the business days by the total days and multiply that fraction by your total travel expenses. Then add the resulting figure to other business travel expenses that appear on your tax return.

Example: Your total of days spent in foreign travel is 20. You spent 12 days on business (as we just defined it). Total expenses were $4,000. Your deductible travel expense is 12/20 times $4,000 which equals $2,400.

EXPERT ADVICE

Plan your trip so that you have business days on Friday and Mondays. Use some Tuesdays, Wednesdays, or Thursdays for vacationing. That makes the weekends into business days, so you may more easily keep your vacation days below 25 percent, and that will make all your expenses into business expenses.

Taking Along Your Spouse or Friend

If the person accompanying you has no business purpose for being there, you can deduct only your costs of travel (and then only 50 percent of your meal costs). However, note that *your* costs are not one-half of the trip's cost. Your costs are what it would have cost you had you traveled alone.

Example: A single hotel room would cost you $90, but you take along your spouse and stay in a double that costs $110. Your deductible hotel expense is $90, *not* one-half of the $110 total.

EXPERT ADVICE

When you fly on business, try to latch onto one of the airline deals that let you take along a friend for one dollar.

Exceptions to This Rule

If your spouse is employed by your employer and would serve a business purpose in accompanying you, his or her travel would also be fully deductible. What is a business purpose? Tagging along just to get your coffee and keep some papers filed wouldn't pass. Being involved in and knowledgeable about products or services about which you are going to make a presentation and helping you in the presentation probably would fly.

If you entertain one or more individuals and the entertainment passes the deductible entertainment tests, and if those individuals bring their spouses to the dinner or other entertainment, then the presence of your spouse might be considered essential to the business purpose. In that case, his or her travel expenses would also be deductible.

Travel As Education

In the good old days, if you were a professor of Greek culture, you could try, and perhaps succeed, in deducting the cost of a trip to Greece for your own education. Sorry, but those days are gone. The tax law no longer allows deduction of travel as a form of job-related education.

Records to Keep

If you want to be able to deduct your transportation and travel expenses, good records are essential. The IRS does not specify what it requires in your records, but they should contain the following:

- Your odometer readings if you use your own vehicle.
  - When you start your trip (from your office, if you go by there first; otherwise, from your home).

- • The start of business travel each day, when you are in a distant city or town, and the end of business travel. By elimination, this will indicate how many personal or "vacation" miles you traveled.
- • When you leave your hotel and start home, as well as your mileage when you arrive home or at your office (wherever you stop first).

- • A list of business calls you make. Just as for your transportation in your home area, an appointment book in which you record appointments made and time spent at each would be sufficient. If you spend the whole day at one location, as a branch store or other operation, note that in your appointment book or mileage log.

- • A record of expenses: lodging, meals, tips, supplies, and so on. The best record occurs when you use plastic for your expenses. The bill from the credit card company is your record. But there are some things that are difficult to charge—some tips, taxis, fast-food lunches, and the like. Note those for which you paid cash in the margin of your appointment book. Remember that the IRS regulations require that the expenses and other items (such as mileage) be recorded at or about the time they occurred. Scribbled marginal notes of expenses are far more likely to be believed than a neatly penned or typed record that appears to have been made after the fact.

- • Receipts for *all* lodging expenses and for other expense items that exceed $75. Again, a credit card record may suffice, but you'll be on firmer ground if you also keep the copy of the charge ticket.

EXPERT ADVICE

Does the $75 figure mean you don't need to keep receipts for expenditures of less than $75? Technically, yes; but I recommend you keep them for everything except the tips to porters, bellhops, and the like and for the fast-food lunches. (You obviously had to eat somewhere, and you can't do it for less than the cost of fast food, so a receipt is superfluous.)

What the IRS Allows for Meals, Even If You Don't Keep Expense Records

You can obtain a detailed list of cities and the meal allowances by calling the IRS at 1-800-829-3676 and requesting Publication 1542, which is free. (The rates are also available on the Internet at http://www.tss.gsa.gov and at http://www.state.gov.)

Do not misread this heading. Even if you neglect to keep records of the cost of meals and incidental travel expenses, you still have to keep a log or diary about mileage, appointments, where you were, and what you did.

The IRS publishes a list of cities and the amount you are allowed for daily meal expense in each one. The daily figure is known as the Federal Per Diem Rate, and varies from $30 to $42 per day. While you are traveling, you can deduct that number as meal expense and forget about writing down what you actually spent.

The IRS list also includes per diem rates for lodging that you may be able to use instead of actual expenses. Using those requires that you be reimbursed by your employer for the travel expenses and that your employer accept the IRS numbers as the documentation for your expenses. (There is more on employer reimbursement in Chapter 4.)

Entertainment Expense

These rules used to be simple: You could entertain a customer, client, or other business contact and deduct the cost. Then the media drew attention to the "three-martini lunch deduction," so Congress felt pressed to change the law. The goal was commendable: Make legitimate entertaining deductible but outlaw the abuses. The result, though, is a hodgepodge of new laws and other complications.

Although the IRS is interested in the nature of the entertainment you are deducting, it is more interested in how and why it had a business purpose and how much you spent for what expenses.

To add to the confusion, the law and the IRS set up two tests, one of which must be passed if you are to legally deduct the cost, or part of the cost, of the entertainment.

Directly-Related-to-Your-Business Test

To pass this test, you need to be able to show that:

- The main purpose of the entertainment was the active conduct of business.
- You engaged in a business discussion with the person you were entertaining *during* the entertainment.

- You had more than a general expectation of getting a business benefit or income from the entertainment.

If you took your customer to lunch but you were unable to discuss business with him or her because of circumstances beyond your control, you can still claim an entertainment deduction. (Maybe the restaurant caught fire, there was a riot outside, or your competitor was sitting at the next table, well within earshot.)

The entertainment that most easily qualifies and passes this test is a quiet business meal during which you can carry on a bona fide presentation, contract negotiation, or otherwise discuss business. In fact, the IRS considers that entertainment where there is distraction cannot be considered *directly related* entertainment expense.

So, if you entertain at a nightclub, theater, sporting event, or a social gathering such as a cocktail party, the IRS considers that you have not engaged in entertainment that is directly related to your business. Also, the IRS considers that entertainment on hunting or fishing trips, yachts, or pleasure boats is not directly related to your business. While you can argue specific circumstances with the IRS, the burden of proving that the entertainment was directly related to your business is on you. (A variation of the guilty-until-proven-innocent rule that operates only in the taxation area.)

If you do not pass this "directly related" test, does that mean that you are out of luck as far as a deduction is concerned? Not really, for you may qualify for the other category, which is:

Associated-with-Your-Business Test

- The entertainment needs to directly precede or follow a substantial business discussion. If the entertainment takes place on the same day as the discussion, the IRS says that meets the "directly precede or follow" requirement. If the entertainment is on a different day, you need to have good reasons for that situation.

    Example: You entertain business associates and their spouses from out of town on the night before or the night after the business meeting. The IRS says it would accept this as "directly preceding or following" a business discussion.

- The discussion must be substantial, but it does not have to be longer than the entertainment. However, the discussion must have a goal of obtaining business or gaining some specific business benefit.

Lavish Entertaining

The IRS says that entertaining that is lavish entertaining is not deductible. What is lavish entertaining? There are no rules other than that the facts and circumstances determine what is lavish. If you do spend an unbelievable amount on an entertainment event, put a memo in your file that explains why you need to entertain in this manner. Thoughts you might include in the memo: Keep up with the entertainment your competitors provide, very large order is at stake, only form of appropriate entertainment available in locality, and so on. (No guarantee here that these points will preserve your deduction, so use your own creativity.)

Conventions As Entertainment

Here, amazingly, is one place the IRS gives you the benefit of the doubt. If you attend a business convention or a meeting sponsored by a trade or business association, the IRS presumes you have met the requirement for a substantial business discussion. The sponsoring organization must schedule a program of business activities that is the main thrust of the meeting, and obviously you must attend the activities.

In other words, if you meet a business associate at a convention, or take him or her there, and invite that person to dinner, you probably will have little argument from the IRS when you treat the cost of the dinner as entertainment expense.

Your Spouse (or Significant Other) at an Entertainment Function

Based on the rules we have covered, you might think that the expenses of your spouse or your business associate's spouse attending an after-business entertainment would not be a legitimate deduction. Thankfully, this is not the case. The law says the spouses must have a business reason for attending, and in this case the IRS does interpret the law realistically. Here's the scenario that works.

Example: Your customer is happily married and always includes his or her spouse in evening activities. When you invite your customer to the dinner theater, you obviously have to invite the spouse. Because the customer's spouse is included, you must include your spouse. Believe it or not, you actually get to treat the expense of all four people as entertainment expense. (Provided, of course, that the dinner theater meets the "associated with" test we have already covered.) Technically, the IRS says that the entertainment of both spouses is an ordinary and necessary business expense.

Percentage Limitation of Entertainment Expense

As for meals while traveling, only 50 percent of entertainment expense (meals *and* shows, night clubs, etc.) are deductible. Watch your computation if part of the expense does not qualify as deductible entertainment expense.

Example: You entertain a client and spouse, and you take your spouse. You also take along your brother-in-law, who has no business reason to be there. Here is the right way to compute your tax deduction:

5 people entertained at $100 each	$500
Subtract one person not business-related	100
Business entertainment expense	400
Subtract 50 percent	200
Deductible expense	$200

In other words, deduct the nonbusiness expense before computing the 50 percent reduction.

The same principle holds true if your employer reimburses you for part of the entertainment expense:

5 people entertained at $100 each	$500
Subtract one person not business-related	100
Business entertainment expense	400
Subtract: Employer reimburses you	150
Your entertainment expense	250
Subtract 50 percent	125
Deductible expense	$125

Double Deduction of 50 Percent of Meal Expense?

I can hear the creative juices flowing in your mind now: If, while on a business trip, you eat dinner with a customer, you think you can deduct half of your meal as entertainment expense and the other half as meal expense. Don't! Congress slammed the door on this maneuver by specifically prohibiting it in the tax law.

Exceptions to 50 Percent Reduction of Meals and Entertainment Expenses

Most of the exceptions to this rule apply to employers only, so they are covered in Chapter 5. The few exceptions (when you can deduct 100 percent of entertainment expense) that apply to individual employees are these:

- Entertainment expense for attendance at a charitable fund-raising sports event if:
  - All proceeds are donated to the charity, and
  - The event uses volunteers for substantially all the work performed.

EXPERT ADVICE

In your appointment book, diary, log, or other record, be sure to note the time the business discussion took place, how long it lasted, and what was discussed. Be specific as to subject matter. A notation of just "business discussion" is sure to motivate an IRS agent to disallow your deduction.

Entertainment Facilities

Facilities such as yachts, hunting and fishing lodges, homes in vacation areas, and so on are not considered business assets, and so the expenses (including maintenance, utilities, depreciation) of these items cannot be deducted. However, when you entertain in one of these facilities, you can deduct the direct expenses of that entertainment. Example: You own a sport fishing boat on which you take a customer fishing. Assuming you meet the tests for entertainment (business-related discussion, etc.) you can deduct 50 percent of the cost of fuel, ice, and food for that trip.

This travel and entertainment area is one in which IRS agents look for gold. As you record your activities, keep expense records, and write down your automobile mileage, try to think like an IRS auditor. Would you believe it? Would you be able to punch holes in your records, find inconsistencies, and determine that your expense deductions are far too high? Thinking that way, rather than just complying with the letter of the regulations, can save you many tax dollars.

Conclusion

Despite the rules and more rules, arguments with the IRS in this area have always happened and always will happen. I hope this chapter will help you in your battles. The next chapter covers more employee business expense and how best to handle reimbursement from your employer.

4

More Business Expense and Employer Reimbursement

WHO SHOULD READ THIS CHAPTER

- Every employee who incurs business-related expenses

- Everyone who is self-employed (and they should also read Chapter 5)

- Every employer who hires employees who incur business-related expenses

THIS CHAPTER INCLUDES

- When you can deduct the costs of gifts to customers and other business associates

- Membership dues you can deduct

- How to deduct your business education costs

- How to make sure you can deduct many moving expenses

- The job-seeking costs that can be tax deductions

- The right—and the wrong—way to be reimbursed by your employer

FAST FORWARD

Job-related Expenses ➤ *pp. 51–58*

It costs money to hold down a job. Here's a rundown on the specific expenses. If you arrange for your employer to reimburse you for expense rather than raising your salary to cover them, you will save more tax dollars.

- Tools, some uniforms, some work clothes, computers, telephones, and so on. These are deductible, at least for the portion of them used for your employer's business.
- Social club dues and expenses. No longer can you deduct these. (The bill for the business meal at your club may be deductible, though.)
- Professional licenses, professional society dues, and union dues. These are still deductible.
- Continuing education in your trade or profession. These costs are still deductible. Other education is not deductible as a business expense, but see Chapter 2 where we cover the fringe benefit of employer-provided educational assistance for any undergraduate study.
- Moving to a new job location. There are several technical rules and limits on the dollar amounts you can deduct.

The Costs of Looking for a Job ➤ *p. 59*

There are several deductions for anyone in the employment-seeking category.

- Résumé preparation, mailing, and telephone expenses.
- Out-of-town travel and local transportation needed in job search.
- Employment agency fees you paid.

Reimbursement of Expenses by Your Employer ➤ *pp. 60–64*

How this is handled by your employer can make a big difference in how much of your job-related expenses you can deduct. General rule: Your employer should reimburse the exact amount of specific expenses rather than giving you an expense allowance.

It does cost money to work. You have to get to work, and you have to return home. You have to buy work clothes. Whether they are tailored suits or jeans and a T-shirt, they do cost money. You may have to personally own various tools. You may need to enroll in an educational program in order to keep up with technology. And the list could go on for many lines.

Some of these expenses can be deducted from your income before calculating your income tax. Some cannot be deducted. Some can be deducted only if they meet certain requirements.

This chapter covers the rules and requirements. It covers more situations than the average working person will run into, so read what's under the headings that apply to you. Some situations may not apply to you because your employer picks up the tab. However, as is the case for many employees, you may have to pay all or part of the job expenses yourself. Even if your employer does pay all of certain expenses, read about them anyway. You can then realize what grief your employer is saving you by keeping the expense records and paying the tariff.

Gifts to Customers

Gifts are somewhat like entertainment, for they are designed to be goodwill builders. However, there are separate rules for deducting the cost of gifts to business associates.

Annual Deduction Limit of $25

You can make a gift of any amount or value to anyone you choose, but you can deduct only $25 of that gift, and then it must be to a business associate. (There is no *income tax* deduction for personal, other than charitable, gifts.) You can't get around this limit by having your spouse, partner, or employer make part of the gift. Such a maneuver does not double the $25-per-associate limit. Normal wrapping and shipping charges do not need to be considered in computing the $25 limit. (If you are on a tax year that is other than a calendar year, the limit is figured on your tax year.)

Trinkets (Specialty Advertising Items)

You can get a 100 percent deduction for any amount of key chains, calendars, pens, and similar items that you give to customers and prospects as long as the cost of each is $4 or less. The items should be imprinted with your name or your employer's name. (You do not need to keep track of how many you gave whom, because these items do not enter into the $25-per-person annual gift ceiling computation.)

Tickets to Theater or Sporting Events

If you accompany the recipient, the tickets are not a gift but entertainment, so the entertainment rules (in Chapter 3) apply.

If you do not accompany the recipient, you have a choice. You can treat the tickets as a gift, which is subject to the $25 limit, or you can treat them as entertainment.

Signs, Display Racks, Promotional Materials

These are not gifts, so no limitation applies to their deductibility.

Dues for Memberships: Deductible?

Most dues are no longer deductible. Here's a rundown on the nondeductibles and the few dues that are deductible:

Dues for Social Clubs Are Not Deductible

This category includes country, golf, athletic, airline, hotel, yacht, and business clubs. By business clubs, the IRS appears to mean clubs that are organized to provide meals "under circumstances generally considered to be conducive to business discussion."

Note that it is the *dues* that are not deductible. Although you can't deduct the $100 you have to remit to the club every month, you can take a business associate to lunch and deduct 50 percent of the cost of the lunch as entertainment—provided it meets the entertainment tests of "directly related to" or "associated with" business.

Dues That May Be Deductible

Business leagues, trade associations, chambers of commerce, boards of trade, real estate boards, professional organizations (the likes of bar or medical associations), and civic or public service organizations. (This last category would be clubs such as Kiwanis, Rotary, Optimists, Lions, etc.)

Notice that the heading to this section said "may" be deductible. This is because the rules state that if any of these clubs are organized for the principal purpose of providing entertainment or entertainment facilities to its members, the dues are not deductible; that is, do not suggest that your Kiwanis Club purchase a sport fishing boat!

Uniforms, Tools, and Similar Business Expenses

Special apparel is deductible if it is required by your occupation and isn't adaptable to general use. That covers safety shoes, helmets, work gloves, and similar items. Questions arise as to whether uniforms are suitable for general use (if so, the cost is not deductible) or not. Advertising, company name, and similar words on a uniform has helped some people win this battle with the IRS.

Other deductible items are small tools and supplies, briefcases used for business, and similar items.

Education

Do you have trouble keeping up with your job? Who doesn't in today's technological world? Keeping yourself educated on up-to-date methods and machines may mean more school. Indeed, many professions require continuing education. If you don't complete X number of hours of continuing education every year, you lose your qualifications to practice your profession.

Fortunately, this further education in your employment field is a deductible expense. It can be the cost of a book you read at home, magazines devoted to your profession, night classes at the local college, seminars related to professional knowledge and management of your business or practice, as well as full-time school. Note the requirement, though, that the education must be to enhance your skill in your current trade or profession.

What if you take courses or otherwise spend money to educate yourself in a new profession? Now you have no tax deduction. That education is considered a personal expense. A promotion is not necessarily a new profession. A lawyer who is promoted from associate to partner has not changed professions, but a promotion from administrative assistant to attorney would be a change of profession.

What Can You Do to Turn Nondeductible Education into Deductible Education?

- Does your employer offer an education fringe benefit? You may be able to effect the same end as a tax deduction by receiving a nontaxable education fringe benefit. (See Chapter 2.)

- As soon as possible, change your education from the status of "new career" to "continuing education." You do that by moving to a job in your new career, so your education will then be improving your skill in your (now) present job. Example: You want to be a CPA who specializes in tax work. Take only the minimum accounting and tax courses that qualify you to take the CPA exam and, we hope, pass it. Get a job as an accountant and now take the advanced tax courses. They now should be classified as continuing education and, therefore, deductible.

Moving Expenses

There is no tax deduction for moving your belongings from one home to another if the reason is personal. It does not matter whether you are moving next door or to Siberia. However, if you move because of a job location change, some of the moving expenses may be deductible. This is so whether you move to a new location with your present employer or the move involves a change of employer. (You can even move and find the new job after you move.) This moving expense deduction applies, with some variance, to both employed and self-employed individuals.

There are some specific conditions that you have to meet in order to deduct certain moving expenses.

Distance Requirement

Compute the distance between your old home and your old job location. The distance between your old home and the new job location must be at least the first distance plus 50 miles. You can use this worksheet to make this computation:

Worksheet

Distance between old residence and new job, in miles   _____

Subtract distance from old residence to old job   _____

     Difference   _____

If the difference is at least 50 miles, you have passed the distance test.

See Chapter 5 for help in determining whether you are an employee or self-employed.

Time Test

The time test varies, depending on whether you are an employee or self-employed.

Employees: Time Test for Moving Expense Deduction

If you are employed by someone else, you must be employed full time in the new location for 39 weeks during the 12-month period starting with your move. You can change jobs during this period as long as the total of full-time jobs adds up to 39 weeks.

If you become disabled or lose your job, you are considered as passing this test, even if you do not find another job.

CAUTION

If you are fired for willful misconduct or just quit your job, this disability and laid-off rule does not cover you. You will still have to find another job and fulfill the 39-week test.

Self-employed Individuals: Time Test for Moving Expense Deduction

If you are self-employed or become self-employed after moving, you must work full time for 78 weeks out of the 24 months starting with the move, and 39 of those weeks must be in the first 12 months.

Moving Costs That Are Deductible

- Traveling expense for you and members of your household. This obviously includes spouse and kids, and it also includes anyone (not necessarily related) who lives in your household before and after the move. But it does not include domestic employees (maid, chauffeur, etc.) unless they are also dependents.

  Members of the household may travel together or separately.

  If you use your automobile to move some or all of your household, you can deduct either the IRS's *generous* allowance of 10 cents per mile or actual out-of-pocket expenses. The latter would include gas, oil, and incidental repairs (e.g., flat tire). You cannot deduct depreciation for this use of an automobile. (This is another inconsistency in our tax rules!)

  You can deduct lodging expense during the travel to the new location, but not meals.

- Costs of packing, crating, and moving household goods and personal effects. This includes cost of shipping your car if you do not drive it. Shipping your boat? You should be able to deduct the cost. Although the IRS may disallow that expense, some courts have ruled against the IRS and allowed the deduction.

EXPERT ADVICE

Deduct the cost of shipping the boat. The fact that courts have ruled that this is legal should protect you from a negligence penalty, even if the IRS strikes that deduction from your computation. (Of course, you still have the right to fight the IRS in court.)

- Storage and insurance of household goods and personal effects for up to 30 days before you move into your new home. You can store the stuff at either your old or new location.
- Disconnecting and connecting utilities (but not telephone).

Moving Costs That Are Not Deductible

- Travel for domestic help (unless he or she is also a dependent)
- Meals
- Trips to new location to search for a place to rent or buy
- A place to live temporarily (such as a motel) while you search for a place to live
- Expenses of buying or selling a home
- Fixing-up expenses of your old home to aid in selling it
- Loss on the sale of your home
- Costs of purchasing a new home

If you have not moved for employment reasons for several years, you will be surprised by this partial list of nondeductible expenses. Many of them used to be deductible, but that is no longer the case.

However, when the Congress and the president take away a tax break, they sometimes (not often) replace it with another tax break. They partially did that in this moving expense area, as covered in the next section.

Where to Deduct Moving Expenses

Deductible moving expenses are no longer an itemized deduction. Rather, these expenses are deducted from your salary and other income to arrive at adjusted gross income. In English, that means that you can now deduct moving expenses and still take the standard deduction, which is good news to many people who rent their residences. For high-income people, it means that the moving expense deduction survives the high-income phase-out of itemized deductions. Use Form 3903 to compute your moving expense deduction.

Reimbursement of Moving Expenses by Your Employer

If the company that employs you reimburses you for the expense of moving from one location to another, it can do it in one of two ways.

Nonaccountable Plan

Your employer gives you a lump sum to cover your moving expenses. The total of that sum is handled just as if it were additional salary and will show up in the total of salaries and wages on your W-2. You deduct the deductible moving expenses on your tax return. (Use Form 3903.) The other moving expenses are treated as personal, nondeductible expenses.

Accountable Plan

You provide a list of your expenses to your employer, presumably on a special company form. Your employer reimburses you for the expenses you paid and may also pay some of the expenses directly (for example, to the moving company). Your employer will prepare and give you an IRS Form 4782, Employee Moving Expense Information. You don't file this form—it's for your information.

Reimbursement of Deductible Expenses Line 1 of this form indicates the amount of money your employer reimbursed you for deductible moving and storage of household goods and personal effects. Line 2 displays the reimbursement for deductible travel and lodging expenses. Both lines 1 and 2 are based on the receipts you give your employer and expenses it paid directly to the service supplier. Your employer should not include these figures in the "salary and wages" on your W-2, although they may be noted in another box on that form for information only. Because these reimbursements are not included in income, you do not deduct them from income. In other words, if you are fully reimbursed for the deductible moving expenses, the transactions surrounding your moving do not appear on your tax return.

What if your employer's reimbursement does not fully cover your deductible expenses? Then you include a Form 3903, Moving Expense, with your tax return. On this form you list your deductible moving expenses and subtract your employer's partial reimbursement. The difference is the figure you can deduct on your tax return as "moving expense." If you prepare your tax return manually (not recommended), you can find filled-in examples of these forms in IRS Publication Number 521. (It's free. Call 1-800-829-3676.)

Reimbursement of Nondeductible Moving Expenses In line 3 of Form 4782, your employer should display the total of any reimbursements for nondeductible moving expenses. This number is added to your regular pay for the year and included in the "salary and wages" box on the W-2.

Gross-up of Moving Expense Reimbursement If your employer reimburses you for only the amount of nondeductible expenses, the reimbursement will fall far short of covering your expenses because you have to pay income tax and Social Security taxes on that reimbursement. For that reason, some employers will "gross-up" the reimbursement so it is large enough to cover not only the moving expenses but the taxes on the reimbursement. Note that this is a transaction between you and your employer, and the details do not appear on any tax form other than the reimbursement included on your W-2.

Searching for Employment? Deduct These Costs

In order to be deductible, these costs must be for a job search in your usual line of work:

- Travel to potential employers
- Résumé preparation, mailing, and long-distance telephone expense
- Employment agency fees
- Other expenses involved in job hunting

Reimbursement of These Expenses

Of course, if your new employer reimbursed you for any of these expenses, you cannot deduct those for which you were reimbursed.

Where to Deduct Job-search Expenses

Unfortunately, these expenses are deductible only as miscellaneous itemized deductions, and they are subject to the 2-percent-of-adjusted-gross-income subtraction. (See "Travel Expenses," the earlier discussion of this sneaky way the government collects extra tax.)

Employer Reimbursement of Transportation, Travel, Entertainment, and Gift Expenses

Congress has, who knows why, rigged the tax law so that it is far preferable that your employer reimburse you for specific expenses than simply providing you with an expense "allowance." The reason is that these transportation, travel, entertainment, gift, and other business expenses that you pay out of your pocket are deductible only as "other itemized deductions." To explain, we'll have to jump ahead and discuss "itemized deductions," which are covered more fully in Chapter 10.

Itemized deductions consist of certain expenses under the headings of medical, taxes, interest, charitable contributions, casualty losses, and job expenses/other miscellaneous deductions. At this point, we are interested in the last category: job expenses and other miscellaneous deductions.

Any deductible business expenses that, as an employee, you pay out of your own pocket you deduct in only one place on your tax return: under miscellaneous deductions. Is that bad? Yes it is, because the tax rules require you to add these T&E expenses to other miscellaneous expenses (such as tax preparation help). Then, from that total you must subtract 2 percent of your adjusted gross income. Only what is left is deducted from your income. (For details and a definition of adjusted gross income, see Chapter 11.)

Example: Suppose your adjusted gross income is $100,000 and you are single. You have spent $15,000 on travel, entertainment, and other business expenses, for which your employer, Skinflint Corporation, does not reimburse you. We'll suppose you rent your quarters and have no other deductions. When you compute your taxable income and tax, it will look like this:

Skinflint does not reimburse, but pays you a salary of $100,000.

Adjusted gross income		$100,000
Computation of deductible business expense:		
Total business expense	$15,000	
Subtract 2% of $100,000	2,000	
Deductible business expense		13,000
Taxable income		87,000
Federal income tax		$21,973

On the other hand, if Skinflint reimbursed you for your business expenses, based upon your submission of receipts to the accounting office, and paid you only $85,000, you would still have the same cash in your pocket as you would in the unreimbursed example above, but your income tax on the $85,000 would be $21,353, which is $620 less than if Skinflint pays you the larger salary but does not reimburse you for expenses.

How to Avoid This Ridiculous Erosion of Legitimate Business Deductions

You can have more of your salary left for you. If a business (as opposed to an individual employee) incurs these T&E expenses, it can deduct 100 percent of that expense. (How's that for Congressional nondiscrimination—only employ*ees* get hit with this 2 percent nonsense.) In other words, if your employer paid your expenses, he or she could deduct all of them. Therefore, try negotiating a change of arrangement with your employer.

Instead of your paying the T&E expenses, submit the bills and receipts to your employer and let him or her pay them and take a 100 percent deduction. Will your employer jump at the opportunity to do this? Probably not—unless you offer to take an offsetting cut in salary. In this example, do you need to take a full $10,000 cut? No, because your employer will save $765 in Social Security taxes when he or she cuts your salary by $10,000. Note that in addition to the $765 your employer saves, *you* also save $765 in Social Security taxes.

CAUTION

Before you ask for a cut in salary and reimbursement of expenses, take a look at your pension plan and where you stand with Social Security credit. If you are in your high-income years and approaching retirement, the higher salary (versus expense reimbursement) may pay off in terms of a higher pension and Social Security benefits. Check your computations with a financial planner before taking this action.

If your salary is lower and under the Social Security maximum base ($65,400 in 1997), there is even a larger gap in the above computation, as that extra $2,000 of taxable income is also hit by the Social Security tax.

If your income is *substantially* higher, there is a far greater advantage in having your employer reimburse you or directly pay your T&E expenses. The reason: Itemized deductions gradually disappear from your tax return if your adjusted gross income increases above $121,200. That means you may have a deduction for T&E of zero! (See Chapter 11 for more explanation of this phaseout of itemized deductions.)

Accountable Plans

For the second method to work, when your employer (not you) takes the T&E deduction, the employer must reimburse employees under an "accountable" reimbursement plan. That means that you submit to your employer a list of actual T&E expenses, and your employer pays you that exact amount.

Reimbursement by Federal Per Diem Rates As an alternative, your employer could pay you the federal per diem rates for travel, as covered before under "Travel." (Note that there is no per diem rate arrangement for entertainment. You do have to have a record of actual entertainment expenses, as well as records supporting the fact that the entertainment was directly related to or associated with business.)

Example 1:

You work as a sales representative for the Pointed Pencil Company. On Tuesday you drive 100 miles to East Overshoe and call on customers in the area. You stay in a motel on Tuesday night, call on more customers on Wednesday, and return home Wednesday night. You compile a list of your actual expenses:

Tuesday meals	$ 32.87
Motel	85.57
Wednesday meals	45.92
Automobile mileage (500 @ 31.5 cents)	155.00
Total	$319.36

You submit this list to your employer and receive a check for exactly $319.36. That $319.36 is *not* added to your wages on your W-2.

As an alternative, if your employer is agreeable, you could submit a list like this:

Meals, 2 days @ federal per diem rate of	
$30 per day	$ 60.00
Lodging, one night at per diem rate	50.00
Total	$110.00

Then you would receive a check for exactly $110.00, and it also would *not* be included in your W-2.

Why would you accept $110 instead of $319.36? If you did not keep expense records and receipts, the $110 is all you could be reimbursed. Moral: Keep expense records.

Remember, even if you use the per diem method for expense reimbursement, you still have to have records of mileage (odometer readings) and business calls you made.

Example 2:

You make the same trip to East Overshoe, but before you leave, your employer gives you $400 to cover expenses. If you spend less, you keep the extra money. Sound good? It may not be, for you.

It's a mixed blessing for your employer. He or she pays you more than needed but gets to deduct the $400 on the company's tax return. Why? The $400 is added to your pay that shows up on your W-2. You get to pay income tax on the $400. Of course, you can deduct your travel expenses on your individual tax return, but you run into the 2 percent of gross income bugaboo we covered a few paragraphs back.

DEFINITION

The first example portrays an "accountable" reimbursement plan. The second is an "unaccountable" reimbursement plan. Generally, you will be better off under an accountable plan as in Example 1.

Where to Find More Details on Entertainment and Business Gifts

If you do a lot of business entertaining or you entertain in some unusual manner, you can call the IRS publications office at 1-800-829-3676 and ask them to send you Publication Number 463, Travel, Entertainment, Gift, and Car Expenses. It's not recreational reading, but it has much detail under specific headings. And it's free.

Conclusion

This chapter covered what are the most common—and most troublesome—expenses of holding a job as an employee. If you are self-employed, there is additional information for you in the next chapter.

CHAPTER

5

What You Pay Yourself— Income from Your Own Business

WHO SHOULD READ THIS CHAPTER

- Everyone who owns his or her own business, either entirely or with other owners

- Everyone who works as a contractor rather than as an employee

- Everyone who is thinking about leaving the ranks of employees and starting his or her own business

THIS CHAPTER INCLUDES

- Ways in which you can organize your business —corporation, partnership, sole proprietor— and the tax implications

- Business income—what it is, where it is, and how big the tax bite is

- How to take cash out of your business without falling into a trap

- Who pays the tax on business income

- Fringe benefits—from an employer's view: pension plans for small companies, things you can deduct that are not taxable to an employee

- Fringe benefits for yourself—tax-free from your own business

65

FAST FORWARD

What Happens When You Hire Yourself ➤ pp. 67–83

- How should you organize your business to pay the least tax? Sole proprietorship is the easiest but not always the best. A regular corporation is straightforward and easy to understand but can involve double taxation of income. S Corporations, partnerships, and limited liability companies are complex but often result in a better tax picture, because they generally pay no income tax but pass the income through to the owners of the business.

- When you hire yourself, you can provide yourself with various fringe benefits, but you have to offer the same fringes to almost all employees, and you are denied some because you do own the business.

- A retirement plan is the most significant fringe benefit. You can avoid relying heavily on expensive consultants by using an IRS-approved prototype plan, available from banks, insurance companies, mutual funds, and other financial organizations.

If you are your own employer or own part of your employer, there are more IRS rules with which you should comply, and these additional rules mean you need to pay more attention to tax planning. You may own a small part of your employer as a junior partner in a professional partnership, or you may be the founding partner and own most of the business. Perhaps you own all of your employer, which might be a corporation or simply your own sole proprietorship. For each of these situations, the rules can be different, so tread cautiously.

Organization Forms That Allow You to Hire Yourself

What follows is an overview of various business organizations and how they are taxed, along with a comment as to when they might fit your needs—from a tax standpoint.

Sole Proprietorships, the Easy Way to Go

This form is the easiest, but not always the best, way to hire yourself. Basically, you hang out a shingle and sell your products and services to customers. You add two forms to your tax return (well, sometimes it's three or four forms). On one of them (Schedule C) you list your gross income (sales, usually) and subtract expenses such as rent, telephone, insurance, wages to your employees, truck or automobile, and depreciation on equipment (more about that later). If you sell products (e.g., a retail store), you deduct the cost of what you sold—*not* what you paid for all the stuff on your shelves.

Then, subtract the cost of the stuff you sold ("cost of goods sold") and the expenses from your sales. That gives you the net profit that is copied to the front of your Form 1040, thereby increasing your income so that you can pay more tax! Use the other form to compute the Social Security tax that you must pay on the income from your business, and that tax is added to the income tax computed on your Form 1040.

It's important to realize that you do not pay tax on the cash you take out of the cash your business generates. You pay it on the computed figure (net profit), as explained above.

Example: This can be illustrated by the sad example of Baron's Beach Ball Store. When Baron opened his store, he took all the money he had ($10,000) out of his mattress and bought 2,000 beach balls at $5 each. At the end of the summer he found he had sold only 500 balls at $12 each. He also paid rent of $500.

Baron assumed his tax picture looked like this:

Sales. 500 balls @ $12	$6,000	
Expenses:		
Bought 2,000 balls at $5	$10,000	
Rent	500	
Total expenses		10,500
Loss		–$ 3,500

Thinking that because he was out $3,500, Baron did not pay any income tax. Then, a year later, the friendly IRS examiner showed up and made this computation:

Sales	$6,000
Minus cost of the beach balls sold at $5 each	2,500
Gross profit	3,500
Subtract rent expense	500
Taxable income	3,000
Income tax (lowest bracket of 15%)	$ 450

Thinking that he owed no tax, Baron had spent the little bit of money from his sales for food and such essentials. Yet, the IRS was displeased and promptly added penalties and interest onto the $450, as well as the Social Security tax, so that Baron owed much more than $450 to the IRS.

Note that Baron still has 1,500 beach balls on hand. That's an asset—something of value that he owns. (Hopefully, he can sell them next summer.)

While large sole proprietorship businesses do exist, they are most often a small operation that started because the owner picked up some tools (or sat at his computer) and built or repaired something that someone else would pay for. As long as the income is in the range of a middle-income job and the owner takes most of the profit for living expense, it is a simple business form that serves the purpose without any undue tax disadvantages.

General Partnerships

Can two people set up a sole proprietorship? By definition, no. Not even a husband/wife team can be a sole proprietorship. Two or more people operating a business (or investment) are a general partnership unless they take positive action to be something else. The "general" preceding "partnership" indicates that all partners are individually liable for the debts of the partnership.

For tax implications, partnerships can be thought of as a group of sole proprietors, for the taxable net profit is computed in the same manner as for a sole proprietorship. The difference is that the partnership net profit is divided between the partners. Each partner pays income tax on his or her share of that taxable income.

This computation of net profit and how it and other items are allocated to partners is done on a Form 1065. Then, for each partner, a Form K-1 is prepared which lists what that partner should report on his or her income. If you receive such a K-1, be aware that the partnership files Form 1065 and a copy of each Form K-1 with the IRS, and the IRS's computer checks to see that you included that partnership income on your individual income tax return. (Big Brother *is* watching!)

If as a partner you are active in the business, you also pay Social Security taxes on this taxable income. If you are not active in the business, your share of the taxable income is not subject to Social Security tax.

When you receive your K-1 from your partnership, look it over carefully. The K-1 does contain notations of where to put which item on your individual income tax return. If you are using good tax preparation software, you will probably find a separate input screen for K-1 information. If you key in the numbers properly, the software should put the numbers on the correct form.

Actually, partnerships can become quite complex, as partnership agreements can allocate various income and expense items in various percentages to various partners. Also, corporations and partnerships can be partners in other partnerships. Unless your business life is extremely complex, there is little need to worry about this much sophistication. Remember, though, that some limitations on tax dodges that apply to one partnership also may apply to other partnerships that are "related."

DEFINITION

"Related" means that there is some degree of common ownership, a partnership is a partner in another partnership, or two family members are partners in different partnerships, or some similar type of interrelationship exists.

Following are two specific types of partnerships with attributes that are specifically authorized in most states. The tax result is that the flow of certain tax items may be different than they would be in a general partnership.

Limited Partnerships

These are partnerships in which only one (or a few) of the partners has personal liability for the debts of the partnership. The other partners are "limited partners." Their liability is limited to only their investment in the business. Generally, they are silent, investing partners. For tax purposes, all partners share the responsibility of paying tax on their share of the income, just as in general partnerships. Also, certain items of income and expense are passed to the partners without losing the character of the item.

Partnership Trap: Flow-through of Specific Items

Sometimes the benefit of a deduction will be lost to certain partners. See what happens to Arnold in the following example:

Example: Arnold and Bubba operate their gutter repair business as a 50-50 partnership. The totals on their bookkeeping records look like this at the end of the year:

Total sales		$100,000
Subtract:		
Wholesale cost of gutter material	$20,000	
Expenses (rent, truck expense)	10,000	
Total subtractions		30,000
Taxable income from operations		70,000
Charitable contributions made by partnership		6,000
Bottom line income		$64,000

Arnold and Bubba would each receive a K-1 from the partnership, listing his share of income from operations as $35,000 (50 percent of $70,000) and his share of charitable contributions as $3,000. Each, on his individual tax return, would insert the $35,000 on the line labeled "Rental real estate, royalties, partnerships. . . . Then, on Schedule A, Itemized Deductions, each would list $3,000 as a Gift to Charity.

In other words, each partner does get the benefit of his share of the $6,000 they donated to charity, but that $6,000 item does not lose its character when it passes through to the partner. (See Chapter 10 for discussion of itemized deductions.)

DEFINITION

"Pass through" is the term used to describe this odd bit of tax rules. The partnership made the contribution, but the amount and the nature of the disbursement "passes through" to Arnold and Bubba.

However, it turns out that Arnold has no other itemized deductions, so he takes the standard deduction on his tax return. That means he loses the benefit of the partnership's charitable deduction. (This is another nefarious way our government hides secret taxes from us.)

If you are an owner of all or part of a partnership, plan ahead. In this example, Arnold would have been better off if the partnership had distributed the $6,000 in cash to the partners and then each partner had made a decision as to when and how much to contribute to charity.

Limited Liability Companies

These are partnerships in which all partners have limited liability for the partnership debts. In that aspect, they resemble corporations, yet they are taxed as partnerships (if they adhere to various IRS rules).

Corporations (C and S)

You have probably heard that, when you set up a corporation, you can create either a regular corporation or an S corporation. However, there are some inaccuracies in that statement. Your corporation would be created by a state authority (upon your application) and, at that point, would carry no designation as either regular or S.

If you take no further action, your corporation will operate as a regular corporation, which is technically referred to as a C corporation. If you apply to the IRS right away and meet certain qualifications, your corporation will be designated as an S corporation. (This type of corporation is also known by the old term of "Subchapter S Corporation.")

C Corporations

C corporations exist as separate tax-paying entities. They compute taxable income and pay the resulting tax directly to the IRS. Stockholders incur no tax liability because of the corporation's earnings, although they do pay tax on salaries they receive if they work for the corporation and on dividends the corporation pays the stockholder(s). (C corporations can be owned by one or thousands of individuals.) This is the type of corporation that can get whammied with a double tax, as follows:

Double Taxation of Corporations This can best be explained by an unfortunate example.

Example: Charlie and Dorothy form a corporation that conducts business during its first year that results in taxable net profit of $200,000. In order to conserve cash, they take no salaries during the year. Then, in December, they find that they both need money, so they declare a dividend of $55,000 payable to each of them on December 20. Also, they are both, because of income earned by their spouses, in a 28 percent tax bracket. Here are the taxes the corporation, Charley, and Dorothy pay:

Corporation taxable net profit	$200,000	
Dividends paid (2 × $55,000)	110,000	
Net profit reduced by dividends	$ 90,000	
Corporate income tax on $200,000		$61,250
Dorothy's tax on $55,000 dividend		15,400
Charlie's tax on $55,000 dividend		15,400
Total tax on the $200,000 net profit		$92,050

As is obvious, the income tax is levied on net profit computed *before* subtraction of dividends. The effective tax rate on the corporate profit is $92,050 ÷ $200,000 = 46 percent!

Dorothy and Charlie could have avoided this result if they had paid themselves salaries during the year. Unlike dividends, salaries legitimately paid to stockholders who are also employees are an expense that can be subtracted from sales in computing net profit. However, large corporations, not all of whose stockholders are also employees of the corporation, have to live with these high tax rates. (The combined corporate and individual tax rates at the highest levels add up to 77.6 percent!)

Incidentally, there is no pass-through of items with special character (e.g., charitable contributions) as there is for partnerships. C corporations take their own deduction for a contribution and are subject to different limits than are individuals.

S Corporations

These are often referred to as partnership-like corporations, and that appellation is partly true. A profitable S corporation that is operating a bona fide business pays no corporate tax. Instead, the net profit (not necessarily the amount of cash distributed) flows to the stockholders and on to their income tax returns. Like partnerships, some items (e.g., charitable contributions) retain their character in the stockholder's hands.

There are some significant differences between S corporations and partnerships.

- S corporations can have no more than 75 shareholders. Partnerships can theoretically have an unlimited number of partners.
- While agreements between the partners (preferably written) control the division of taxable profits, that is controlled by state corporation laws and federal tax laws for an S corporation.

- If an S corporation was ever a C corporation, it could find itself paying some corporate taxes of its own. This is due to tax laws that prevent the avoidance of tax on previous C corporation earnings by electing S corporation status.

- There are other technical differences. Suffice it to say that even if you prepare a corporate or partnership return yourself, you should at least have a tax professional review the return.

The reporting of S corporation income is similar to the reporting of partnership income. An S corporation reports it on a Form 1120S rather than a partnership form, but like a partnership it also prepares and reports each stockholder's share of the income and other items on a Form K-1.

The same trap that is described in the Arnold and Bubba example under partnerships operates for S corporations. Again, be careful.

Taking Cash Out of Your Business

This is, of course, what all the strain of operating a business is about—generating cash that you can enjoy. Here's the rundown on how and when.

Sole Proprietor

If the cash is in your business and you need it personally, you can just take it out without tax consequence. (It's the net profit that generates tax, not the cash withdrawals.) That's not a good budgeting procedure, but the tax man isn't concerned with that.

Partnerships, Limited Partnerships, and Limited Liability Companies

In a simple partnership, the effect of distributing cash to partners is similar to a sole proprietorship: There is no tax generated. However, if some partners have their interest in the business by virtue of buying the partnership interest from someone else, or if there has been a history of losses, distributions of cash could trigger taxes for some partners. (Technically, it happens if the distributions exceed the partner's basis in the partnership. Hire some professional help if you have this situation.)

The Cash Trap That Can Ensnare Partners

Finding out that you owe income tax and have no money with which to pay it is not only embarrassing, it's downright expensive in terms of the penalties and interest that the IRS will add to the bill. See the example under cash distributions from S corporations that follows.

C Corporations

Never just write a check to a stockholder. If he or she (or you) is also an employee, take the cash out in the form of salary. Withhold income tax and Social Security and report the wages to the IRS, just as you would for any employee.

If you write a check for an unspecified purpose, the IRS will assume it's a dividend and taxable—and that's double taxation.

As an alternative, the corporation can make a loan to a stockholder. However, the loan must have a due date (which should be honored), be in the form of a formal note, and, if the loan is over $10,000, market-rate interest must be charged and paid. (Nine percent should keep you out of trouble.)

Do not overlook expense reimbursement. Be sure to reimburse yourself for any business expense that is legitimate, including travel and entertainment that meet the tests in Chapter 3.

S Corporations

Like C corporations, you can write checks to stockholders for salary, expense reimbursement, and loans. If you write a check without specifying what it is for, the IRS will expect you to treat it as a distribution, which would have a tax consequence only if the distribution exceeded the stockholder's basis. (You can find that number on the stockholder's latest Form K-1, explained later in this chapter.) Note this: Distributions to stockholders not in proportion to their stockholdings may violate your state's corporation statutes.

Social Security Impact on S Corporation Stockholders

Unlike partnerships, a stockholder's share of S corporation taxable income is not subject to Social Security taxes. But the corporation is expected to pay reasonable salaries to the stockholders who work for the corporation, and those salaries are subject to both Social Security and income taxes.

EXPERT ADVICE

Small S corporations are sometimes set up to dodge Social Security taxes. Instead of paying salaries to stockholders who are active in the corporation, the corporation pays out only distributions of "previously taxed" income, which escapes Social Security tax. Before you try that, remember that the IRS has the power to change the character of the numbers on a tax return. In other words, it could change all of the "distributions" to "salary," causing a significant unpaid Social Security tax and penalties. Better bet: pay as small a salary as is reasonable for the work performed by employees who are also stockholders. Then there is a basis for argument with the IRS: Are the salaries reasonable? If no salaries are paid, there is no basis for argument.

Cash Distributions Trap That Can Ensnare Partners and S Corporation Stockholders

Here is what happened to some partners who did not plan their cash flow:

Example: Nikita, Mao, and Fidel own the common stock of an S corporation, called Rampant Capitalism, in these percentages.

Nikita	30%
Mao	10%
Fidel	60%

Evita, the corporation's accountant, computes its taxable income to be $1,000,000. She sends a Form K-1 to each stockholder, telling her or him how much income she or he has to report on his personal tax return. (Nikita must report and pay tax on income of $300,000; Mao, the same on $100,000; and Fidel, the same on $600,000.)

Notice that I said that Evita divides up the taxable income *number,* which does not mean she divides up the *cash!* Fidel decides the corporation should not distribute any cash to the stockholders but should keep the money in the corporate bank account for use in expanding its business. (It doesn't matter what Mao and Nikita want the corporation to do. Fidel owns more than half of the stock, so he controls the corporation.)

Fidel has a few hundred thousand dollars stashed in his mattress, so he easily pays the tax that he owes on the taxable income of Rampant Capitalism, Inc. However, Nikita is strapped. He has only $1.97 in the bank, but he owes $130,000 in tax on his share of the corporation's income. He pleads with Fidel to cause the corporation to divvy up some of the cash among the stockholders, but Fidel refuses. (Such is gratitude for past favors.) Nikita is in trouble. He not only loses sleep; he also loses his house, car, boat, and other assets that the IRS grabs and sells to pay off his tax bill.

EXPERT ADVICE

If you become a stockholder in an S corporation and you own less than 51 percent of the stock, be wary of this situation. Insist on an agreement that the corporation will always distribute enough cash to the stockholders to enable them to painlessly (?) pay the income tax.

This scene can also occur in partnerships, so the same advice is applicable to partners.

Withdrawal of Inventory and Other Assets for Personal Use

For all forms of business, taking inventory off of the shelf and taking it home or taking an office chair home for your den is the same as taking cash. For business forms except C corporations, it presents only a bookkeeping task. However, for C corporations, the IRS may view it as a dividend, and then you're into the double taxation situation.

Wages and Salaries to Other Family Members

For any small business, this can be an effective tax-saving tool, regardless of the form of the business. It can divert profits that otherwise go on your tax return (at high rates) to children or retired parents who are taxed at lower rates.

In order to be legal, the recipients should perform services that have value. In other words, they should really work and earn the wages they are paid. For children under age 14, this would be earned income, so it is not subject to the Kiddie Tax (covered in Chapter 11). Obviously, you can't put a two-year-old to work on anything that merits paying a wage, but older children can be put on the handle end of a broom for starters. If you have a teenager who is a computer whiz and you need a computer consultant, hire the child and pay consulting rates. It could finance the higher education.

CAUTION

Before you divert substantial funds to a child this way, check on its effect on his or her eligibility for financial aid for college.

Health Insurance Coverage by Your Business for Your Family

There is a special rule for sole proprietors, partners who own more than 2 percent of a partnership, and S corporation stockholders who own more than 2 percent of the stock. If you fit this description, you can deduct 40 percent of your health insurance cost (in 1997) on your Form 1040. The good news is that this is not an itemized deduction but a deduction you can take even if you use the standard deduction.

The percentage of deduction increases each year until it reaches 80 percent in 2006, and it is also limited to the amount of self-employment income you have. (For S corporation stockholders, that is the total amount of their salaries. It does not include distributions.) The deduction is not available if you or your spouse is covered under some other employer's medical plan.

There is another method of deducting health insurance and other medical expense: Install a health and accident plan in your business to cover employees. Hire your spouse in your business so he or she would be covered, and you and your children would also be covered as the spouse and children of a covered individual. If you have other employees, do make sure you meet the nondiscrimination rules for health and accident plans. (Your source for the insurance coverage should be able to help you meet that requirement.)

The Tax-Free Room and Board Fringe Benefit

This tax break is not available to a sole proprietor who lives on the site of this business. The reason: no employer-employee relationship exists. The IRS takes the position that this tax-free benefit is also not available to partners, even though the partnership requires a partner to live at the business. However, several courts have ruled against the IRS in various cases. If the money involved warrants it, obtain some aggressive professional help and take the deduction.

If your business is incorporated, it may be a little easier to set up a bona fide employer-employee relationship. If you want to be aggressive in labeling your lodging and meals as "for the convenience of the employer," take these actions at least:

- Have a written agreement between the corporation and you, the stockholder. The agreement, however, should refer to the parties to the agreement as "employer" and "employee", not as "corporation" and "stockholder."
- Prepare a written job description of the employee (you), citing the requirement and the necessity for the employee to live and eat on the premises.
- Draw a regular and reasonable paycheck from the corporation. (Treat it like any paycheck—withhold income tax and Social Security taxes.)
- Hold a board of directors meeting in which the directors authorize this arrangement, and record this action in the minute book.
- Have an aggressive tax professional review these documents.

Retirement and Savings Plans in General

As a business owner, however, you have more options than you do as an employee, for you get to choose the plan that your company offers, and you also get to worry about the IRS's approval of the plan. (If you do not have IRS approval, you cannot be certain that you can legitimately deduct your contributions to the plan.)

If you have many employees, it is foolish to select and install a retirement plan without professional advice. However, if your only employee is yourself or you and your spouse, you can find a bank, insurance company, mutual fund company, stockbroker, or other financial institution that offers standard IRS-approved plans.

Plans that cover employees can also cover yourself, so you can sock away tax-sheltered money in addition to providing an employee benefit in your company's compensation package. Unfortunately, though, there are limits to how much you can allocate to yourself, and they vary with the type of business form in which you conduct your business.

Earned Income Requirement

For all of the following, only *earned income* is eligible for the base on which to compute the retirement plan deduction.

Example: Margaret runs a plumbing company, installing plumbing in new houses. That business earns a taxable income of $50,000. She has owned an office building for many years, and it generates a taxable income of $100,000. For her own retirement account, she can contribute only $6,522 (13.0435% × $50,000). The $50,000 from the plumbing business is considered earned income. The rental income is not earned income, so she cannot use the $100,000 to compute her maximum contribution to her own pension plan.

Nondiscrimination Rules

These rules prevent you, as an owner of the business, from adopting a retirement plan, making most of the contributions for your personal benefit, and deducting the yearly cost of the plan. The rules are complex. Unless you use a plan already approved by the IRS, you should retain a professional who specializes in this area to guide you.

Sole Proprietorship

Operating as a sole proprietor, you can set up almost any plan that can be set up by corporations and other forms of business. However, due to a complication in the law, the limit on your contribution is lower than it would be if you were an employee of a corporation. Specifically, your contribution has to be deducted from your self-employment income before the deductible contribution can be computed. Some mathematical minds have computed this to be 15 percent instead of the usual 13.0435 percent. The contribution for the owner does not escape Social Security tax. Taxable income of the proprietor is computed, and Social Security tax on that number is computed before the retirement plan contribution is deducted from income. (Remember, even if your earnings are over the FICA tax limit, the hospital insurance portion of Social Security applies to *all* earned income.)

General Partnerships

The same rules that apply to sole proprietorships apply here. Although the plan is installed by the partnership, each partner takes the deduction for the contribution to his or her retirement account on his or her individual income tax return. Partners also have the same limitation on contributions (13.0435 percent).

As to whether there is earned income on which to base a retirement plan contribution, each partner is considered individually. Does he or she work in the business and earn the income, or is the partner an investor, earning investment income on which contributions cannot be based?

There is an exception to special rules for partners: Those who own 10 percent or less of the partnership are not treated as owner-employees but as regular employees. Therefore, the limit on contributions to their retirement is the 15 percent limitation.

Limited Partnerships

If you are a limited partner (investor), your share of any taxable income is not *earned* income. You didn't do any work to *earn* it, so you are not eligible to participate in a retirement plan.

Limited Liability Companies

In most cases, the general partnership rules apply.

C Corporations

As for contribution percentages and other rules, owners (stockholders) of C corporations are treated the same as other employees. However, the management has to be careful that the nondiscrimination rules are followed.

S Corporations

Owners (stockholders) are treated the same as partners in a partnership. As for partnerships, those owning less than 10 percent are treated like any other employee.

Types of Plans

These can be any of the plans discussed in Chapter 2, where they were covered from an employee standpoint. However, there are plans for small employers which are subject to fewer IRS rules and therefore simpler to install and administer.

Simplified Employee Pension (SEP) Plan

This is a plan in which the employer makes contributions to each employee's IRA. The maximum contribution is 15 percent of an employee's compensation or $30,000, whichever is lower. The rules include some hurdles to jump through to make sure the plan does not discriminate in favor of highly compensated employees.

Salary Reduction SEPs (SARSEPs)

These are SEPs to which contributions are made by each employee. The employee elects either to have his or her salary reduced and the equivalent amount put into an IRA or to take the full salary in cash. These plans have not been allowed since 1996.

SIMPLE Retirement Accounts

These can be adopted only by employers with 100 or fewer employees (excluding those who earn less than $5,000 during the year). This is the "cash or deferred" plan that replaced the SARSEP. The SIMPLE plan does not have as many rules to follow, such as rules that prevent discrimination in favor of highly compensated employees. However, the maximum contribution by an employee cannot exceed 15 percent of compensation or $6,000, whichever is higher. There is also a requirement that the employer make contributions for each employee who has elected contribution to this retirement plan instead of cash. (The employer contribution can be no more than 3 percent of the employee's compensation.)

Defined Benefit Plan

This is the classic pension plan. Put away money now and you will receive X dollars when you retire. It's administratively burdensome, but in certain circumstances it may be worth it. Specifically, if you are in your 50s, want to salt away as much as possible for retirement, and have the cash flow to do so, installing a defined benefit plan in your business could greatly increase your annual contribution limit. But be careful. If you have many other mature people in your employ, you will have to make large contributions to their accounts. On the other hand, if you have no other employees, or if your employees are all very young, this could work for you. Check it out with a professional who specializes in retirement plans.

How Do You Choose a Retirement Plan for Your Business?

You probably should get professional help for this, but before you do, think about your goals:

- How much do you want to put away into a retirement plan for yourself? How much can you afford to put away?
- How much do you think is appropriate to spend for a benefit for your employees? (What do you have to do to attract the best?)
- Are you in your 50s and want to sock away as much as possible in the next few years? If you have no other employees or only much younger employees, think about a defined benefit plan. Because you are older, you should be able to contribute more tax-deferred funds to your account than to the account of a younger employee.
- If you are younger and able to put away a limited amount of money, a SEP or SIMPLE plan may be the best and the least expensive (administratively) for you.

Should You Become Self-Employed?

This chapter should have provided enough tax information to help you make this decision if you are not already among the ranks of entrepreneurs. Before you decide, read more. There are whole books devoted to this subject.

Income from Investments in Securities

WHO SHOULD READ THIS CHAPTER

- Anyone who does not need to spend every penny he or she makes
- Individuals with investments of any kind
- Those who are saving for the future
- Retired individuals who are living on the income from their investments

THIS CHAPTER INCLUDES

- The tax on interest income, from banks, the government, stocks, and mutual funds
- Tax-exempt interest explained—when it's good and when it's bad
- Dividend income—it's usually taxed, but sometimes it isn't
- Mutual funds and the resulting taxes you pay

FAST FORWARD

Income from Interest-bearing Investments ➤ pp. 87–96

- Interest income, unless it comes from tax-exempt state and local bonds, is taxable. No longer can you defer income tax on interest with zero coupon and other deferred interest bonds. You have to pay tax on the computed interest, whether you were paid it or not.
- Installment sales generate interest income, whether you like it or not. Again, the IRS says you must compute it if it's not stated.

Dividend Income ➤ pp. 97–98

- Dividends come in different flavors. Don't pay too much tax on capital gain or nontaxable (return of capital) dividends.

Investments come in many sizes, flavors, and methods by which they are taxed. This chapter is devoted to income from securities and bank products. The next chapter covers gains and losses when you sell securities.

By way of review, securities historically consisted of fancy pieces of paper indicating that the person who held the paper was a part owner of a corporation (stock), was a creditor of a corporation or some government unit (bond), a partner in some venture (usually real estate), or had a right to buy or sell any of the foregoing at some price. Now, of course, much of the paper has been replaced with electronic data files (which is somewhat scary). These, then, are what we cover in this chapter.

Income from Interest-bearing Investments

With few exceptions, interest you receive is taxable income, and it comes with almost no tax breaks. Here's a rundown:

Accounts in Banks, Credit Unions, Savings and Loan Associations, and Similar Institutions

Whatever interest you earn on these accounts goes directly to your tax return. It makes no difference whether you withdraw the interest in cash or leave it in the account. Some institutions name the earnings on your account "dividends," but for reporting on your tax return, follow this rule: Report them as whatever the 1099 you receive says they are. (A 1099-INT reports interest you earned, whereas a 1099-DIV reports dividends.)

Interest from Bonds Issued by Governments

Federal Government Issues

Bonds and other debt instruments issued by the federal government have one significant advantage (besides their safety): For the most part, interest income on federal debts cannot be taxed by the states. The most common federal government debt issues are Treasury bills, notes, bonds, and savings bonds. Here is a rundown on how they are taxed.

Series E and EE bonds You have an option with these bonds.

1. You can wait and report the interest over the life of the bond when you cash in the bond, which you can do at any time, but be sure to do it no later than when the bond matures; or

2. You can report the interest every year you hold the bond.

Because the interest accumulates in the value of the bond, you receive no cash payments of interest until you redeem (cash in) the bond. Therefore, on the face of it, option one is more appealing. (Option two requires that you find other cash with which to pay the tax on the savings bond interest.)

However, if you intend to use the proceeds of the bond for a child's education, buy the bond or transfer ownership to the child and pay the tax every year at the child's low rate. Generally, this works only if the child's unearned (investment) income is less than $1,300 or the child is age 14 or over. (If the child doesn't meet either of those tests, the Kiddie Tax provisions come into play, and those say that your child pays tax at *your* rate, not his or hers.) Of course, you will have to find the cash elsewhere to pay the annual tax—not from cashing in a bond. If you transfer bonds you own to your child, be sure you have the transfer documented in the government's records by having the bond reissued in the child's name.

Similarly, if you are in a no-tax or low-tax bracket and expect much higher income in later years (e.g. if you are a student), you could make this election to report interest every year. However, once made, the election is binding on all savings bonds you own now or in the future.

CAUTION

Before you rush out to buy savings bonds for your child (or transfer existing bonds you already own), consider what happens to college financial aid eligibility if your child owns the bonds in his or her own name. Also, consider the section of the tax law that allows you to cash in Series EE bonds for educational purposes without paying any income tax. To do that, these conditions must be met:

- *The bond must have been issued after December 31, 1989.*
- *The individual to whom they are issued must be age 24 when the bonds are issued. (If you are just turning 24, be aware that bonds are issued as of the first of the month in which you purchase them.)*

CAUTION *(CONTINUED)*

- *The bonds must be Series EE.*
- *The proceeds from cashing in the bonds must be used for tuition and fees (not room, board, and other expenses). Scholarships must be deducted from tuition and fees before computing how many EE bonds can be cashed in during the year.*
- *The proceeds must be used for the owner of the bond, his or her spouse, or a dependent. Note that this won't work for a grandparent's buying the bond for a grandchild, unless the grandchild is a dependent of the grandparent rather than the parent.*
- *The educational institution must be post-secondary public and non-profit private institutions. Technically, they must qualify for federal assistance under the Higher Education Act of 1965 or the Carl D. Perkins Vocational Education Act. For-profit schools do not qualify.*
- *For 1997, you must file a joint return with adjusted gross income of less than $76,250 or, if you're single, less than $50,850. You can still get partial benefit of this provision until it phases out completely at figures of $106,250 for a joint return and $65,850 for a single return. (These numbers are adjusted annually for inflation.)*

If you exclude interest income for this purpose, complete Form 8815 and enter the total from that form on Schedule B of Form 1040.

If you have made the election to pay income tax annually on the interest on these bonds, make sure you do not pay tax twice. When you cash in the bond, you will receive a 1099-INT from the federal treasury department. For that form, the government computes the taxable interest income as if you had never reported any of the income. What do you do? Copy the interest figure from the Form 1099-INT to a line on the "interest income" section of Schedule B. Then add up the interest from this bond on which you paid interest in previous years. Enter that on the last line of the "interest income" section, calling it, "Minus previously reported U.S. savings bond interest." Subtract that from a subtotal of interest income for a net total in the interest income section, which is the figure carried to page one of Form 1040.

There is more flexibility in these bonds. If, when your Series E or EE bonds mature, you intend to use the cash proceeds to buy more government bonds, do not follow that route. Instead, exchange the bonds for Series H or HH bonds. You will receive interest on the latter bonds every six months, and the IRS will expect you to pay tax every year on that interest. However, the accumulated interest on the E or EE bond that you traded in does not get taxed until you finally cash in the H or HH bonds, or until they mature. In other words, you can defer that tax on the E or EE bond for as much as another 30 years.

Treasury Notes and Bonds These are simply government IOUs that twice a year pay interest that is taxable. The government will send you a 1099-INT at the end of the year, reminding you to include it in your taxable income (on Schedule B).

Treasury Bills These are issued with maturities of 12 months or less. No interest payments are made, but you buy the bills for less (the "discount") than the amount you will receive when the bills mature. You report that discount as interest income when the bill matures, even if you bought it during the previous year. However, if you sell the bill before its maturity, some of the discount may be capital gain. That happens if the difference between the face amount of the bill, minus your original cost, prorated for the time you held the bill, is less than your gain when you sell the bill.

Example: You buy a $10,000 treasury bill for $9,700 and sell it 85 days later for $9,875. Your computations would look like this:

Face amount of bill	$10,000
Original cost of bill	9,700
Interest if held to maturity	300
Daily interest ($300 ÷ 180 days) 1.667	
Sale price of bill	9,875
Original cost of bill	9,700
Total gain	175
85 days' interest at $1.667 per day	142
Capital gain	$ 33

Observation: Unless you have some capital loss you need to offset with capital gain, this computation may not be worth your time. If it isn't, report the entire $175 as interest income.

Bonds Issued by State and Local Governments

The most significant aspect of these is that the interest is not taxable by the federal government and often is not taxable within the state of the local government that issued the debt. Because investors who buy these bonds do not have to share the interest income with the IRS, they are willing to accept a lower rate of interest on these tax-free bonds.

Should you avoid taxes by buying these bonds? That depends on your tax bracket (the rate at which you would pay income tax on the interest). You may find that you are ahead to buy a taxable bond (which would pay a higher interest rate) and pay the tax on the interest.

How do you tell which, taxable or nontaxable, bonds would be best for you? Find your tax bracket (as explained in Chapter 11) and then use these formulas:

The nontaxable rate equivalent to a given taxable rate is equal to: taxable interest rate times (1 minus your tax bracket rate)

Example: If you are in the 28 percent tax bracket and can buy a taxable bond paying 7 percent, what is the equivalent nontaxable interest rate?

$$7\% \times (1 - .28) = 7\% \times .72 = 5.04\%$$

If you can find a nontaxable bond paying more than 5.04 percent, buy it instead of the taxable bond. (This assumes that both bonds are of similar quality.)

There is also a formula for the reverse computation: The taxable interest rate equivalent to a given nontaxable rate is equal to: nontaxable interest rate divided by (1 minus your tax bracket rate).

Example: If you are in the 28 percent tax bracket and can buy a nontaxable bond paying six percent, what is the equivalent taxable interest rate?

$$6\% \div (1 - .28) = 6\% \div .72 = 8.33\%$$

If you can find a taxable bond paying more than 8.33 percent, buy it instead of the nontaxable bond. (Again, this assumes that both bonds are of similar quality.)

Bonds Issued by Corporations

If you own coupon bonds, the interest is taxable to you as each coupon matures, whether or not you turn in the coupon for payment when it is due. If interest is paid by the corporation by check, the interest is due when you receive it or have a right to it. (You should receive a 1099-INT that will reflect this.)

Complicated Interest Tax Calculations

If the interest income you receive is entirely from your bank, insurance company, or similar institution, you have probably read far enough about interest income. Just be sure you check the 1099-DIV you receive against the interest you have actually received or that has been posted to your account during the year. Banks do make mistakes, so be sure you don't pay tax on interest you never received.

If your interest-income life is more complicated, you should read on. What would make it more complicated? Our greedy government wants tax receipts *now,* not later. Here are brief explanations of the complexities, with suggestions on what to do if they appear in your financial life.

Original Issue Discount (OID)

This concept is easier to explain with an example: You invest $100,000 in a bond, paying 10 percent interest at the end of each year, issued by the Consolidated Combination Corporation (CCC) and maturing in 10 years. We will assume you are in the 28 percent tax bracket and, to keep it simple (?), live in a state with no income tax.

Each year, you receive the $10,000 interest, pay Uncle Sam the $2,800 income tax on it, and put the rest in a bank where it earns 5 percent interest. At the end of the tenth year, you get back your $100,000 investment and you have $90,561 in the bank, for a total of $190,561.

As an alternative, CCC offered you this before you made your original investment: You need invest only $88,736 at the beginning of the first year and at the end of 10 years, CCC will pay you $230,158. But wait! You have to pay income tax on the interest that is in that figure, and after you stroke the check to the IRS, you have $190,561 left. But this still is a better deal, for you had to invest only $88,736, rather than $100,000.

Why is the alternative better? There are two reasons: First, you have all your money working at 10 percent with CCC. In the original alternative, some of it is earning only 5 percent at the bank. Second, If you pay no income tax until the bond matures, you have all your money working for the full 10 years.

Now that you are excited about the second alternative, there is bad news. This works only in the case of Series E and EE U.S. Savings Bonds. Years ago, it worked for other bonds. Then the IRS came up with the idea that even though interest was not paid on your $88,736 each year, it was *earned* each year. Ergo, it could be taxed each year.

This earned interest, called *original issue discount (OID)*, became taxed. The bonds that are structured this way are generally called *zero coupon bonds*. If you own any of this type of bond, you should receive a Form 1099-OID annually, which will give you the computed interest on which you should pay tax. That form might come from either the issuing corporation or the broker who sold it to you. If you question the computation of the interest, you can order the free IRS Publication Number 1212 (1-800-829-3676), which lists many publicly traded bonds and the OID interest on which you pay tax, as well as more than you ever wanted to know about computing OID interest.

EXPERT ADVICE

Zero coupon bonds are not a sensible investment for those of us who have to pay income tax on interest we won't see for years. However, as an investment vehicle for an IRA or an employer's retirement plan, they do make sense. Why? Of course, you do not pay annual taxes on income within an IRA or retirement plan. More important, your money is fully invested, earning compound interest until the bond matures.

Other Complications and Technical Terms

There are other terms in this bond area. I will mention them briefly, for, like most busy people, if you run into them, you will likely dump your questions and problems on the desk of a tax professional. What follows will help you in deciding if you need professional assistance.

Strips are bonds from which the interest coupons have been removed, or "stripped," and sold to someone else. If you buy a stripped bond, you will pay less than its face value for it (because the coupons are gone), so the stripped bond becomes an OID bond, meaning you should pay tax on the OID interest each year.

Market discount is the result of buying a bond in the marketplace (not from the organization issuing it) at less than its face value. That will result in extra profit when you cash it in for face value at its maturity. Unfortunately, that "profit" will then be taxable as ordinary income.

Premium on a bond results when you pay more than the face amount for the bond. There is good and bad news here: For taxable bonds, the premium can be *amortized* (spread out) over the time until the bond matures, and the annual amortization can be used on Schedule B to offset some of the interest income.

Example: You buy a bond issued by Deadweight Corporation, having a face or maturity value of $1,000 five years from the date you purchased the bond and paying interest at 10 percent. You pay $1,100 for the bond. Your calculations would look like this:

Purchase price of bond	$1,100
Face amount of bond	1,000
Premium you paid	100
Divide premium by number of years to maturity	5
Annual premium amortization	$ 20
Annual interest ($1,000 × 10%)	100
Subtract annual premium amortization	20
Taxable interest income each year	$ 80

You report this on Schedule B of your Form 1040 by listing the $100 of interest income (so it will match the interest reported on Form 1099-INT by Deadweight Corporation). Then subtract the $20 on another line on Schedule B, labeling it "less amortized bond premium."

This amortization also decreases your loss when you sell the bond, as discussed later in the capital gain section of this chapter.

Amortization of premium on a nontaxable bond exists also, but it cannot be used to offset interest income. The bad news is that it increases the gain (or reduces the loss) you may have if you sell the bond in the marketplace before it matures or redeem it at maturity for its face amount. The theory is that, because you didn't have to pay tax on the interest, you should not be able to deduct the loss (your purchase price minus your sale price) from other taxable income. (I didn't say it was a *good* theory!)

Bonds with OID Belong in Retirement Accounts

If you have these bonds in a retirement account, as in a 401(k), you rid yourself of all of these computation problems. Just cash in or sell the bonds and take the cash out of the retirement account (after you're eligible to do so). Then your computation is simple: You pay ordinary income tax on your withdrawals, sometime in the future.

Bond Mutual Funds

This is another easier way to invest in bonds. The experts hired by the funds will do the tax computations and send you a Form 1099-DIV. That form will simply give you total figures to enter on Schedule B of your tax return, including nontaxable income. (Note that even though the fund earns interest from bonds, the income it sends you is a dividend. The significance of that is where you place it on Schedule B.)

Interest from Installment Sales

If you sell something you own to someone else and allow them to pay you in installments, you are actually loaning them some money. (Your buyer has what you sold him or her and owes you the money for it.) Therefore, part of what they pay you in the future months and years is interest, or so the IRS says.

Example: You sell a parcel of vacant land (for which you originally paid one dollar) to Jill Jones for $100,000. She pays you $20,000 down and agrees to pay you $10,000 per year for the next eight years. You will be better off tax-wise if all of that $80,000 she pays you is capital gain than if any of it is interest, because of the lower tax rates on capital gains. But the IRS will not allow you to do this.

What the IRS will do is this: It will compute that almost $19,000 of the $80,000 that Jill will pay you is interest on the loan and that in each of the eight years you must pay regular, high-rate, income tax on that interest as you receive it each year. (The interest is computed by an amortization table, just like you have for your mortgage.)

How do you avoid having the IRS change your tax picture and bill you for delinquent income tax, with the addition of interest and penalties? You structure your sales agreement with Jill to reflect that part of each payment is interest. The safe harbor is to use a 9 percent interest rate in this computation. (Use the loan amortization software you probably have on your computer, or have an accountant make the computation for you.)

You may be able to structure this agreement with a lower interest rate. Specifically, you can use the *applicable federal rate (AFR)* in effect for the month in which you make the sale. Where do you find that? If you use a professional tax preparer, call him or her for the information. If you do it all yourself, the IRS publishes it in the *Internal Revenue Bulletin*, which should be available at large libraries. Perhaps an easier process is to call the IRS at 1-800-829-1040 and ask for the current rate, but don't try to call that number on April 14. All you will hear is a busy signal.

Interest Income on Loans to Others

If you loan money to someone else (including your corporation) and the amount is over $10,000, you should charge interest on the loan. If you fail to do so, the IRS will say that some of what your debtor pays back to you is interest income. You will then find yourself paying tax on the return of your own money!

You can escape that result by charging at least 9 percent or the AFR if that is less.

EXPERT ADVICE

If your loan is to a relative, it is even more important to charge and collect interest, even if the loan is less than the safe harbor of $10,000. Failure to make the loan in a business-like manner will cause the IRS to view your "loan" as a "gift." That would destroy any hope you might have of taking a deduction for a bad debt if your relative fails to pay you back.

Dividend Income

Dividends from Regular Corporations

Except for very small corporations, such as those discussed in Chapter 5, corporations are owned by many stockholders. Each stockholder's share of the corporation is evidenced by the number of shares of stock that he or she owns. Unlike bonds, which pay a predetermined amount of interest, stock certificates represent a share of ownership of the corporation. If you own stock in a corporation, you may receive income in the form of dividends. Future dividends are unknown, as they are paid by declaration (whim) of the board of directors of the corporation, and can take various forms.

Dividends on Common Stock

If a corporation pays the dividend from current or past earnings in cash, it is a taxable dividend, you list it as such in the dividend section of Schedule B, and you pay regular income tax on it. If you sign up for a corporation's program to reinvest the dividends in more of the corporation's stock, you do not escape tax on the dividends. The IRS treats the transaction as if you had received the cash and sent it back to the corporation for the purchase of more stock. The 1099-DIV you receive from the corporation will include this dividend in Box 1.

Dividends on Preferred Stock

Even though preferred stock appears to be like a bond, it is an ownership vehicle. If you have plain vanilla preferred stock, which is entitled to dividends before any dividends are paid on the common stock, report the dividends as you do for common stock, on Schedule B. However, like bonds, dividends on preferred stock can be stripped from the stock. If you own stripped stock or the dividend rights, or if you strip the stock, you will have to wade through the instructions in IRS Publication 1212. Better idea: Ask your broker to recommend an accountant who is familiar with the taxation of these fancy investments.

Mutual Funds (Registered Investment Companies or RICs)

Mutual funds are corporations. Like any corporation, their goals are to earn profits and pay dividends. However, there is a special set of tax rules for these special corporations that allow them to escape corporate taxes. Specifically, they must pass most of the dividend income and may pass the capital gains income on to the owners (stockholders) of the mutual fund shares. So, if you own mutual fund shares, you will undoubtedly receive income from them, and you will have to pay ordinary income tax on the dividends and capital gain tax on the capital gains that are passed on to you.

You can find out how much dividend income and the nature of that income (ordinary or capital gain) from the Form 1099-DIV you should receive. It should be entered in Schedule B of Form 1040.

Real Estate Investment Trusts (REITs)

These corporations are almost identical to mutual funds, except they invest in real estate. Again, most of the income will "pass through" to you in dividend form, and you should receive a 1099-DIV explaining how much to report on Schedule B of your Form 1040.

Other Dividends

From regular corporations, mutual funds, and REITs, you may receive notification that you have received dividends with names like nontaxable dividends, stock dividends, and stock splits. Each of these has little or no impact on your current taxable income, but they do impact the gain or loss when you sell the stock in the corporation. Therefore, you will find them discussed in the next chapter, which is about gains and losses incurred when you sell securities.

Income Tax When You Sell Your Securities

WHO SHOULD READ THIS CHAPTER

- Individuals who own securities
- People who plan to sell some of their securities
- People who want to increase capital gain after-tax income
- Retired individuals who are living on the income from their investments

THIS CHAPTER INCLUDES

- New rules for taxes on capital gains
- How to avoid taxes by timing purchases and sales

FAST FORWARD

Gains and Losses on Securities ➤ pp. 101–109

- Hold your stocks, bonds, and other investments for 18 months for the best tax treatment under the 1997 changes in the income tax law.
- The date of May 7, 1997, is an important capital gains date. What went on before is history. What has gone on since is meaningful.
- Sell investments with losses in time to offset capital gains on investments you have sold or want to sell.
- Don't be tripped up by the old rules on wash sales.
- Don't be tripped up by the new rules on "selling short against the box" and other tax-saving maneuvers.

Although you're probably a trader looking for a fast profit, there comes a time when a company's fortunes change, or the industry changes, or the price of a security is far above reason, so you decide to sell the stock you own in that company. When you sell it and when you sell other securities, it can make a big difference in your income tax bill. The maneuvers to make that happen are in this chapter, and they are based on the changes in capital gains rules made by the Taxpayer Relief Act of 1977. Assuming the long bull market is continuing as you read this, you probably have significant profit in some securities you own. If so, read on carefully. Don't let the tax people get more than a small share of your gains.

Gains and Losses When You Sell Securities or They Mature

First, we need to define a couple of bits of jargon:

DEFINITION

Gain or loss, in English, is the difference between what you originally sold something for and what it originally cost you. Unfortunately, that definition is too easy, so the tax law writers obfuscate it as: *The difference between the amount realized on a sale of an asset minus the basis of that asset.*

DEFINITION *(CONTINUED)*

Amount realized essentially means the same as net sale. In other words, it's the sale price minus commissions, fees, delivery expenses (postage or express), and any other costs of the sale.
Basis is what you originally paid for the item plus or minus various adjustments, such as amortization of bond premium or discount.

Gain or Loss?

Obviously, if the amount realized is more than the basis, there is a gain from the sale. If the basis is more than the amount realized, there is a loss from the sale.

Before proceeding to compute the tax, you need to add up all of your capital gains for the year (both before and after May 7, 1997) and subtract all of your capital losses. If the result is positive (a gain), then the complex new rules on taxation of capital gains come into play. If the result is negative (a loss), the loss rules take effect. (The loss rules are discussed after the tax on capital gain is covered.)

How much tax you pay not only depends on how much gain or loss is involved in your sale, but it also depends on the nature of the gain or loss—is it capital gain or loss (possibly low tax rate) or is it ordinary income or loss (high tax rate). If it's capital gain or loss, which is generally the case with sales of securities, then we need to answer the question of what tax rate applies, and that depends on how long you have held this item. (In 1997, it depends on what *day* you sold the security.)

NEW LAW

Gain on sale of a security

Gain on Sale of a Security Before May 7, 1997

If you sold a security before this magic date, the gain is taxed as in prior years. If you are in a 28 percent or less tax bracket, the tax is the same as on any other taxable income. (See Chapter 11 for help in determining your tax bracket.) If you are in a higher tax bracket (31 percent or more), you pay only 28 percent on the gain *if* you held the security for more than 12 months. If you owned the security for less time, you pay the same rate as on other income, which may be as high as 39.6 percent.

Gain on Sale of a Security After May 6, 1997

The Basic Changes in Rates Are These

- If you are in a 15 percent bracket, your capital gain tax rate for sale of securities you held long enough is 10 percent.
- If you are in a 28 percent or higher tax bracket, your maximum capital gain tax rate for sale of securities you held long enough is 20 percent, and you may find some of your gains taxed at 10 percent.

The Holding Period—How Long Does It Need to Be?

In its haste to give us "simple" tax rules, Congress has come up with the following edicts that apply to sales of securities after May 6, 1997:

- For sales made after May 6, 1997, and before July 29, 1997, the securities must have been held for more than 12 months to qualify for long-term capital gain rates.
- For sales made after July 28, 1997, the security must have been held for more than 18 months to qualify for the long-term capital gain rates.
- There is now a new term in the tax lingo: mid-term gain. This applies to securities sold after July 28, 1997, and held for more than 12 months but not more than 18 months. The maximum rate for these gains is still 28 percent.
- If you held the security for 12 months or less, the gain on the sale is taxed at regular income tax rates, which range from 15 to 39.6 percent.

Confused? Join the club! Suppose you are in a 28 percent or higher tax bracket. Consider a stock you held for 13 months and then sold. If you sold it before May 7, 1997, your highest tax rate on the gain is 28 percent. If you sold it after May 6, 1997 and before July 29, 1997, your maximum tax rate on the gain is 20 percent. If you sold it after July 28, 1997, you are back to a maximum rate of 28 percent. (After July 28, you have to have held the security for 18 months to have the 20 percent tax rate apply.)

Collectibles

If you invest in collectibles, the old rules still apply (maximum rate is still 28 percent, and you must have owned the collectible for more than 12 months).

How to Compute the Holding Period

The holding period begins on the day after you own the security and ends on the day you sell it. Count months, not days. For securities, the date you purchase and the date you sell is the *trade* date, not the settlement date.

Example: If you bought BigGain, Inc. stock on June 30, 1997, to qualify for long-term gain (12 months), you could not sell it until July 1, 1998. If you bought it on March 31, 1998, you need to hold it 18 months for the lower tax rates, so you should not sell it before October 1, 1999, in order to enjoy the lower rates.

Losses on Sales of Securities

If your calculation of subtracting total capital losses from total capital gains resulted in a loss, the rule works this way: If your loss is $3,000 or less, you can deduct that loss from other forms of income (salary, dividends, interest, rent, and so on, usually referred to as "ordinary income"). Through the computations on Schedule D, that loss ends up as a negative figure on page one of Form 1040.

If your capital loss is more than $3,000, you can apply only $3,000 of that loss to ordinary income. Where does the rest of the loss go? You don't lose it, because you can carry it forward to next year and the following years for as long as you live. In the following years you use the loss first to reduce capital gains. As long as you are using the loss to reduce capital gains, the only limit on how much you use is your capital gains. If your loss carryforward has reduced capital gains to zero, you can use another $3,000 of the loss to offset tax on ordinary income.

Example: In 1997, Donald sold his 1,000 shares of stock in BellyUp Corporation for $1,000. He had purchased the stock years ago for $15,000. Because this was his only sale of a capital asset during the year, he has a capital loss of $14,000. He uses it as follows:

Loss in 1997	$14,000
Minus loss used in 1997	3,000
Loss carryforward to 1998	$11,000

In 1998, he did better in the stock market, so his net capital gain for 1998 was $6,000. He applied the loss carryforward from 1997 to offset that $6,000 capital gain, and he used an additional $3,000 to reduce ordinary income. Now his computation for 1998 looks like this:

Loss carryforward from 1997	$11,000
Minus loss used in 1998 ($6,000 + $3,000)	9,000
Loss carryforward to 1999	$ 2,000

In 1999, he would use up the remaining $2,000 of the loss by applying it to capital gains, if he had any, or to ordinary income.

If he had had more capital losses instead of capital gains in 1998, he would have added the loss to the $9,000 carryforward and used $3,000 of that total to reduce ordinary income. Then he would have carried the remaining capital loss balance forward to 1999.

Loss When Stock or Bond Becomes Worthless

When a security becomes worthless, you have the same loss as if you had sold it for zero money. That is, it is a capital loss and is claimed on Schedule D.

Make sure you claim the loss in the year the investment becomes worthless, not when you get around to it or when you can use the loss to offset some gains. This scene explains why:

Example: You bought for $10,000 some common stock in the BellyUp Corporation in 1990. In 1991, the corporation filed for bankruptcy. The bankruptcy was discharged in 1992 (the corporation ceased to exist). Some creditors received what few assets were left, the stockholders received zilch, so your stock became worthless.

You reported nothing about it on your tax return until your 1996 return, when you had some large capital gains from selling some stock in profitable corporations. In 1997, the IRS audits your 1996 tax return. The cheery auditor looks into your deduction of a capital loss on the BellyUp stock.

"Oh ho," she says. "This became worthless in 1992. It can be claimed only on a 1992 tax return."

"No problem," you say. "I'll amend my 1992 tax return and carry the capital loss forward to 1996."

She replies, "No, you won't. That's a closed year, because more than three years have elapsed since you filed your 1992 tax return. You are out of luck and out of a $10,000 capital loss deduction."

Unfortunately, the IRS auditor is correct. How do you guard against this really happening to you? Claim the loss in the first year that you can justify the security becoming worthless. (In the example, I would claim it in 1991. If on audit the IRS objects, just claim the loss in 1992, which usually still would be an open year (a year you could amend).

You can't lose the capital loss once it is claimed on a tax return and the IRS doesn't question it. That loss can be carried forward indefinitely until you have capital gains to offset it. (See Chapter 11.)

Losses on Stock in Small Corporations

There is an exception to the $3,000 limitation on losses that you can deduct from ordinary income. If you are the original purchaser of the stock when it was issued by a "small business corporation," and you later sell the stock or the stock becomes worthless, you can deduct up to $50,000 ($100,000 on a joint return) of the loss from ordinary income. There are several other requirements in Section 1244 of the Internal Revenue Code. If you are involved in setting up a corporation of $1,000,000 or less capitalization, make sure your corporate attorney complies with those requirements. (If he or she doesn't know about Section 1244, find another attorney who does.)

Selling Bonds Can Bring Added Complications

The added complications are in the area of computing basis. Several items discussed earlier in this chapter have an impact.

Bond Premium and Amortization

If you paid more than the redemption price (usually the face amount) of a bond when you purchased it, your basis would be your cost (minus expenses of purchase such as commissions and fees). However, you may have elected to amortize that premium. If so, you reduce your basis by the total of the amortization you deducted from interest income over the years you held the bond.

If you hold the bond until it matures, cashing it in amounts to a sale in which there would be no premium that had not been amortized.

Market Discount

If you purchased the bond from someone who was not the issuer (as in the open market) and paid less than the redemption price (usually the face amount) of the bond, the difference found by subtracting what you paid from the redemption price of the bond is the market discount. That figure is ordinary income when you sell the bond. (If you bought it at a discount from the issuer, that is OID, which was covered earlier.)

There is an escape hatch from having to make this computation and pay tax at ordinary rates. (The buzz word for the escape hatch is "de minimis rule.") Make this computation:

1. Count the number of years until the bond matures.
2. Multiply the redemption price of the bond when it matures by .0025.
3. Multiply the result in (1) times the result in (2).
4. Compare the total market discount to the figure found in (3). If the market discount is less than (3), ignore the market discount. Your entire profit on the sale or redemption of the bond is capital gain.

Example: You bought a taxable bond with a maturity value of $1,000, maturing in 20 years, for $960. Your computations as to whether the *de minimus* rule applied are:

1. Years to maturity   20
2. Maturity value ($1,000) times .0025   <u>2.50</u>
3. Multiply no. 1 by no. 2 $50.00
4. Discount when purchased ($1,000 minus $960)   40.00

No. 3 is larger than no. 4, so the *de minimus* rule applies. Your $40 profit when the bond is redeemed is capital gain.

You could have chosen to include a ratable portion of market discount in your income each year you owned the bond. If you did, your basis is increased by the amount of market discount on which you paid tax each year. In other words, you don't pay tax on the same income twice.

Original Issue Discount (OID)

If you own an OID bond, you should have been receiving a 1099-OID every year, stating the OID interest you should report on Schedule B. When you sell the bond or it matures, add up all of the OID interest on which you have paid income tax and add that total to your original basis in the bond. That figure is now your basis for computing capital gain on the bond.

Dividends That Affect Basis, Gain, and Loss

Nontaxable (But May Be Taxable) Dividends

In some instances, you may receive a dividend that is not paid out of earnings but is a return of the capital invested by stockholders. In that case, you pay no tax on it unless this and all previous "non-taxable" dividends *paid to you* add up to more than you paid for the stock. Any excess is taxable but as capital gain. It therefore goes on Schedule D, not B. These dividends will appear on a Form 1099-DIV in box 1d.

Example: Two years ago, you paid $100 for 100 shares of Leaky Buckets, Inc. Now you receive a "nontaxable" dividend of $150. As this is $50 more than you paid for the stock, you report the dividend as long-term gain on Schedule D.

How can this be? You get back more than you paid for the stock? This scenario would work: You bought the 100 shares from Lou Loser, who bought the stock when it was issued for $5 per share, for a total of $500 that went into the corporation's treasury. The extra $50 that was returned to you was just part of Lou's original investment. (Your gain, his loss!)

Stock Dividends

These usually take this form: For each 10 shares of Foolem Corporation that you own, you will receive a stock dividend of one additional share of Foolem Corporation. If every stockholder is treated alike, this dividend is nontaxable. Why? Nothing except the number of shares of stock has changed. The whole corporation is still worth what it was before the stock dividend. Sure, you have a greater number of shares, but you still own the same fraction of the whole corporation, so your greater number of shares is still worth, in total, what your fewer number of shares were worth before the stock dividend.

Stock Splits

These are nothing more than disguised stock dividends. The split is a nontaxable event, but both stock dividends and stock splits have an effect on the basis of your stock when you sell it.

Reinvestment of Dividends

Most mutual funds permit and encourage you to reinvest your dividends in more shares of the mutual fund. This means that you will have purchased shares at several different times and, most probably, at several different prices. Therefore, it is important that you keep all of your statements from the fund so that you can compute the basis of your mutual fund shares when you sell them.

Other Securities (Derivatives)

Many investment and speculative securities go under the name of "derivatives." Included are stock options, index futures, commodity futures, stock rights, stock warrants, and other securities. There are also hedging tactics that are supposed to defer taxable gain on securities, such as "selling short against the box," equity swaps, covered options, and other esoteric names.

Be aware that, although the derivatives are alive and well, their tax status and the related tax deferral tactics have been attacked by Congress. The 1997 tax law changes include a new provision, titled, "Constructive sales treatment for appreciated financial positions." Which tactics will fly and which won't is unknown, for much of the interpretation must await regulations to be written by the IRS. At this point, suffice it to say that if a broker or advisor suggests any of these tactics to you, hold off taking these tax deferral actions until you can receive advice from a knowledgeable tax professional.

Tax Planning for Your Investments in Securities

Here are some ideas that may lighten your tax burden.

Time Stock Purchases to Defer Taxes

Be aware of ex-dividend dates of stock you plan to purchase. (The ex-dividend date is the date on which the buyer of a stock will not receive a dividend that has already been declared.) If you buy a stock before the ex-dividend date (when it is "cum dividend"), you will soon receive some of your own money back, along with the obligation to pay income tax on your own money!

Example: HighProfit Corporation's board of directors declares a dividend of $4 per share, payable on June 30 to stockholders of record as of June 10. On June 10, the stock trades at $104 per share. On June 11 (the ex-dividend date), it trades at $100 per share. If you decide to buy the stock on the morning of June 10, you have a choice:

Choice #1:

You buy 100 shares of stock on June 10 at $104	$10,400
Shortly after June 30 you receive a dividend check	400
Your net investment	$10,000

Choice #2:

You buy 100 shares of stock on June 11 at $100	$10,000
You do not receive the dividend	0
Your net investment	$10,000

The difference: If you go the choice #1 route, you will incur an income tax liability on the $400 of dividend income. If you wait a day and follow choice #2, you avoid that tax on $400. (Note that the stock market is somewhat logical in this area. If there is no change in the stock price due to other circumstances, the price will drop by the amount of the dividend on the ex-dividend date.)

Of course, there may be some nontax reasons to buy the stock on the tenth (cum dividend date). If there is fast-breaking positive news about HighProfit Corporation on the tenth, so that you think there will be a big price rise during the day, you may be ahead to buy it on the tenth and pay the extra tax.

Cut Taxes by Timing Loss Sales

If you have securities that have increased in value and you think it is time to sell them, search your investment portfolio for securities that have declined in value. Then, sell your losers in the same year that you sell your winners. The losses will offset the capital gains.

Watch Out for Wash Sale Rules

If you sell a security and buy the same security within 30 days, the sale and buy-back did not happen as far as the IRS is concerned. Why? It prevents this sort of tax maneuver:

Example: You own 100 shares of Maybe Corporation, which you bought at $60 per share, but it is now trading at $30 per share, so you have a paper ("unrealized") loss of $30 per share. Because you also have $4,000 of capital gains on securities you have sold this year, you would like to be able to deduct that loss on Maybe Corporation this year, but to be deductible, the loss must be realized—you must sell the stock. However, you expect the price of the Maybe Corporation stock to soar much higher in the next few weeks. So, you sell your 100 shares on December 26, which you think will generate the loss on this year's tax return. Then you buy back 100 shares of Maybe Corporation on January 2, in order to take advantage of the expected price rise.

Sorry. The *wash sale rule* prevents this because these transactions are within 30 days of each other. What if your January 2 purchase was of a different class of Maybe Corporation's common stock? It would not avoid this rule if both classes of common stock were "essentially identical securities."

How can you avoid the rule?

- Make sure there are more than 30 days between the sale and purchase of the stock.
- Make the offsetting purchase of stock in another similar company whose stock price moves generally in the same manner and magnitude as the Maybe Corporation stock price.
- If your expectation of a higher price is based on expecting the stock market as a whole to move up, buy a market index option instead of the Maybe Corporation stock on January 2. Hold the option until the 30-day period has passed, then sell the option and buy the stock back. (No guarantee here that the stock market index will move so as to make this work.)

Tax on Income from Real Estate Investments

8

FAST FORWARD

Income from Rental Real Estate ➤ *pp. 115–132*

Many expenses can be deducted from rental income besides taxes, interest, and depreciation. Keep records of all expenses, including the use of your vehicle to check on properties.

Rental of real estate can often develop a loss on your tax return while you enjoy a positive cash flow. Almost anyone can deduct $25,000 of such a loss, but in order to deduct more you have to be operating a real estate business rather than casually renting a house or two.

A sale of a real estate parcel often creates large capital gain tax problems. Try to legally avoid the tax by arranging a tax-deferred exchange of properties.

Use your vacation property for 14 days or less, rent it to others for as many days as you can, and thereby develop a loss you can deduct from your regular income.

If you follow the rules, you can sell your residence with up to $500,000 in gain and pay no income tax on the sale.

Income from Rental Real Estate

In its simplest form, rental income works like this: You own an apartment building; from each tenant you collect monthly rent, and the total of all the rent is called gross rent. From that, you can deduct various expenses, such as mortgage interest, real estate taxes, other expenses, and depreciation. It all gets reported on Schedule E, Supplemental Income and Loss.

Noncash Rental Income

To be taxable, rental income does not have to be in cash. If your tenant performs services for you or makes improvements to your rental property in lieu of rent, the value of the services or improvements is rental income. However, if the tenant makes improvements to the property for his or her own enjoyment and not as a replacement for rent, the improvements are not rental income. (If the improvements have lasting value, they should generate a higher price when you sell the property, and that will generate tax for you to pay.)

Renting to Related Entities

If you rent property to a corporation that is wholly or partially owned by you, or rent an apartment to your sister, charge *and collect* the going rate for your area. If you charge your corporation too much, the IRS might say that part of that excess rent is a disguised dividend. So, they would recharacterize it as a dividend, making it nondeductible by your corporation. (That amounts to the bugaboo of double taxation of corporate income.) If you charge your sister too little, the IRS would hold that you are making a gift of the apartment use to your sister and would then disallow the part of your expenses allocable to your sister's apartment.

The above situation involves what is the principal residence of your sister. The rules are different for rental of your vacation home, discussed later in this chapter.

Expenses That Are Deductible from Rental Income

Keep track of any and all expenses that are reasonable and necessary to maintain your property and collect rents. The following expenses need some additional comment.

Automobile Expense

Don't forget to keep a log of your automobile mileage and expenses incurred in trips to your rental properties (for collections, maintenance) and mileage to the hardware store and other maintenance-related activities. The rules for computing automobile expense as for a self-employed business (Schedule C) apply.

Interest Expense

This includes mortgage interest on the rental property, plus interest on any additional funds that were borrowed for repair or improvements on the property. Unlike the mortgage on your personal residence, points cannot be deducted in the year you paid them. They must be amortized over the length of the loan.

Example: If you paid points of $2,400 to obtain a 20-year mortgage on your apartment building, you could deduct that interest only at the rate of $10 per month interest expense. ($2,400 ÷ 240 months = $10)

Taxes

Annual property taxes are deductible. Assessments for improvement, such as for a sewer line, sidewalks, and so on, are not deductible. They are in the nature of improvements to the property, so they should be depreciated, as are buildings. (See the depreciation explanation that follows.)

Maintenance

If you perform maintenance on your rental property yourself, you get no deduction for your own labor. In theory, if you wrote yourself a check for $100 of labor, you could deduct the $100, but you would also have to report as taxable income the $100 you paid yourself. So, it's a wash. (Note: that's a theoretical explanation. Don't write that check—just live with the result—it's a wash.)

Here's some tax planning many people miss. Let's say you own your own residence and one other house that you rent out. Both houses need roof repair, and the cost of labor to repair the roofs is $2,000. You're fairly handy, but you don't have enough free time to repair the roof on both houses. Therefore, you do the roof repair on the rental property and pay the Curly Shingle Company to repair the roof on your home. Wrong! You cannot deduct the $2,000 to repair the roof on your residence, for that is considered a personal expense. Neither can you deduct anything for your labor on the rental property, as already explained.

The right way: Do the maintenance on your residence yourself, hire it done on the rental property. Had you handled the roof jobs that way, you would have an additional deduction of $2,000 with no additional outlay of cash.

Depreciation of Rental Property

Basically, depreciation is a method of allocating, or spreading out, the cost of the income-producing asset over the life of the asset. The IRS requires that you depreciate an income-producing asset that will last several years, and to end a lot of arguments, how long and at what rate you depreciate an asset is now fairly well set in concrete.

If you have rental property that you purchased in a prior year, the depreciation system that you set up in the first year you owned the property is the system you continue to use. (If you find that the system, or schedule, was improperly set up or you failed to deduct depreciation, it is possible to change your depreciation deduction in prior years by sending a request to do so to the IRS. I have omitted the details on how to do that, as it is an area for which you should seek professional help. (If you must do it yourself, call 1-800-829-3676 and ask for IRS Publication Number 534.)

Allocating Cost of Property Between Building and Land

Before you make computations of depreciation expense, remember that most rental real estate consists of a building on a piece of land. The building you can depreciate, for it will wear out in time. The land will be around, as far as we know, for several million more years. The IRS considers that means that the land does not wear out, so you cannot take depreciation deductions for it. Do you ever get a deduction for the cost of land under a rental building? Yes, when you sell it, for then the cost of the land is deducted from the proceeds of your sale. (You also can take a loss if you have waterfront land that washes out to sea in a storm.)

If you buy land and construct the building, how much of the value is attributed to the land and how much to the building should be obvious. The cost of the building and costs such as foundation fill, grading, utility connections, and similar costs are usually lumped together under the name of "improvements," and that total is the figure that can be depreciated.

If you purchased existing property to rent out, you have to compute the allocation of your purchase price between the building and the land. The IRS will generally accept this method: Find what percentage of the tax assessment is for land. Multiply your purchase price by that percentage to determine the value of your land.

Example: You buy an apartment building for $300,000. The city or county assesses the value as $60,000 for the land and $120,000 for the building, for a total of $180,000. The land value percentage is $60,000 ÷ $180,000, or 33.3 percent. Multiply the $300,000 you paid by 33.3 percent to find your land cost, which turns out to be $100,000.

Computation of Depreciation

If you bought *residential* rental property after 1987, your building is considered to have a useful life of 27.5 years. If you purchased commercial real estate after May 13, 1993, your building's useful life is 39 years. You might think, then, that you compute your depreciation by dividing the cost of an apartment building by 27.5 to find the annual depreciation deduction. Of course, the IRS does not do things that simply. You start the depreciation in the month you place the property "in service." (That's the month you have the property in shape to rent, whether or not you immediately find a tenant.) Then, the IRS says you must use a "mid-month convention," which means that you get only one-half of the first month's depreciation. From that information, you could compute your depreciation, but there is an easier way.

The IRS has published tables (giving percentage of building cost that can be deducted as depreciation) for each year you own the property. There is a separate column for each month of the first year that the property is put in service. To obtain the tables, call 1-800-829-3676 and ask for the free publication. Table 6 in that publication refers to residential property, and table 7a refers to nonresidential (commercial) property.

Incidentally, this area is one of the stronger arguments for using tax preparation software on your computer. All of these programs do all the depreciation computations for you, based on the same formulas that the IRS uses.

Net Income or Loss from Rental Property

Subtracting all of the expenses (including depreciation) from the gross rental income results in a net income or loss. Through the mechanics of Schedule E, any net income is included in taxable income on your Form 1040. Unfortunately, net losses are another matter. You may or may not be able to deduct these losses from your other income.

Limitations on Net Losses

The rental of real estate (and other tangible property) is a passive activity for most individuals, and passive activity income and loss are a one-way street. You always pay taxes on passive income, but you generally cannot use passive losses to reduce your regular income. (In other words, the IRS always wins. You often don't win!) Passive losses can be used only to reduce passive income.

Example: You own two apartment buildings. The first generates a net loss of $30,000 per year. The second generates an income of $40,000. You can offset the loss on the first against the income of the second, leaving you a taxable income of $10,000.

If you didn't own the second property, that $30,000 loss would stay out in limbo until some year when you have other passive income. (But see the $25,000 exception that follows.) That is, the passive loss is carried forward until you can use it in some year. If you never have needed passive income, you can deduct the accumulated passive loss on the first property when you sell it.

The passive income from which you could deduct this loss need not come from rental; it could also come from a business in which you were not an active participant. (Note that dividends [from a C corporation] and interest are "portfolio income" and therefore you cannot use passive losses to offset this income.)

Exceptions to the Real-estate-income-is-passive Rule

The $25,000 Exception If you have at least a 10 percent interest in a rental real estate activity and "actively participate" in the operation, you can probably deduct $25,000 of that loss even though it is a passive loss. What is the "active participation" you must do? Managing the property, such as approving tenants, determining lease terms, and approving repair expenditures should do it. If you leave all of that to a rental agent, or if you are a limited partner in a real estate operation, you probably do not qualify for this $25,000 escape from the passive loss rules.

Also, this $25,000 escape is not entirely available to you if your adjusted gross income is over $100,000, or $50,000 for a married individual filing a separate return. The $25,000 phases out at the rate of 50 cents for each dollar your adjusted gross income exceeds the $100,000/$50,000 limit.

Exception for Material Participation in Real Property Business Basically, this exception applies if you are engaged full time in activities such as property development, construction, acquisition, conversion, rental, operation, management, leasing, or brokerage trade or business. The specific rules the IRS has laid down to qualify for the "material participation" in a real estate trade or business for a particular year are:

- More than half of the personal service you perform is in a real property trade or business.
- You devote more than 750 hours to the real estate trade or business. If you file a joint return, only one spouse needs to have spent the 750 hours. (You cannot add the times of both spouses together to arrive at 750 hours.)

If you are involved in several real estate activities, you need to qualify in each of the activities in order to qualify for this exclusion from the passive activity loss rules. However, you can elect to have all of your real estate activities grouped together as one business for tax purposes.

Gain or Loss When You Sell Rental Real Estate or Real Estate Used in Your Business

The *basic* concept of gain or loss on a sale of rental real estate is simple, if you are familiar with three terms:

- Amount realized is the price for which you sell the real estate, minus costs of sale, such as commissions.
- Accumulated depreciation is the total of all of the depreciation you deducted since you acquired the property.
- Basis is what you originally paid for the property minus the accumulated depreciation.

Example: On January 1, 1988, you purchased an apartment building for $300,000, of which $50,000 represented the value of the land, so the building cost was $250,000. On December 31, 1997, you sell it for $750,000, with costs of sale (commissions, etc.) of $50,000.

Basis of property:

Original cost		$300,000
Subtract accumulated depreciation		
Annual depreciation (building only)		
($250,000 / 27.5 years)	$9,091	
Times 10 years	× 10	
Total accumulated deprecation		90,910
Basis when sold		$209,090

Gain on sale:

Amount realized ($750,000 minus $50,000)	$700,000
Subtract basis	209,090
Gain on sale	$490,910

The good news: The gain of $490,910 is taxable at capital gain rates, which would be a maximum of 20 percent in this case, provided you sold it after May 6, 1997.

Would that tax life were always this simple. (It was, in 1913.) To explain why it isn't, we have to introduce more terms:

Straight line depreciation is what we used, and you have to use it after 1987 for real estate. It results in the depreciation being the same figure for every month you own the property. (A graph of time versus the amount of depreciation is a *straight line.*)

Accelerated depreciation is depreciation that is faster than straight line. It goes by such appellations as 150 percent declining balance, 200 percent declining balance, sum-of-the-digits, and other words lifted out of accounting textbooks. (Ugh!) Then the IRS added its own terms of ACRS MACRS, and other confusing terms.

In the above example, 150 percent declining balance would have resulted in a depreciation in 1987 of $13,636 (150 percent times $9,091). The second year would be computed this way:

$$(\$250,000 - \$13,636) \div 27.5 \times 150\% = \$12,893$$

Tax software will do these computations for you, so this is more than you really need to know if you use tax software or a professional preparer. Of course, the present depreciation rules would prohibit you from using accelerated depreciation on property acquired after 1986, but it is legal for property acquired before 1987.

What *should* be of interest to you is that, if you have rental real estate that was acquired before 1987, you well may be using accelerated depreciation. If so, not all of your gain on sale will be limited to the top rate of 20 percent; some of it may be taxed as ordinary income at higher rates. You can make the computation of how much gain is so taxed on Form 4797, following the complex instructions for the form. Again, a better idea is to use tax software or a preparer who has tax software.

Remember, also, that if you sell rental or business-use real estate you have not held for the required period (12 months for sales after May 6, 1997, and before July 29, 1997; 18 months for sales after July 28, 1997), the gain is taxed as ordinary income, subject to tax rates up to 39.6 percent of taxable income. If you sold the property before May 7, 1997, and held it for more than 12 months, the maximum tax rate you might pay is 28 percent.

Avoid the Tax Bite On Disposal of Real Estate By Like-Kind Exchange

If, in the preceding example, you did not sell the apartment building, but traded it, even money, for a shopping center, you would pay no tax on the exchange. The basis of the shopping center, in your ownership, would be the same figure as the apartment building ($209,090). For this rule to be applicable, the properties exchanged must be of the same nature, character, or class of property. The grade of quality need not be alike. Real estate for real estate qualifies, but you can't exchange your residence for anything but another residence. Note that this rule covers an exchange, not a replacement. In other words, if you sold the apartment building for $700,000 and immediately bought another property for $700,000, that is not an exchange. The gain on the sale is taxable.

Like-kind Exchange for Property and Money If you exchange your apartment property for a strip shopping center plus $100,000, the transaction is taxable but only to the extent of the cash you received. In the above example, only $100,000 of gain would be taxable. Your basis in the shopping center would be your basis in the apartment building you traded ($209,090) plus the $100,000 on which you were taxed, or $309,090.

Mortgage on the Property Traded If you owned the apartment building free and clear, and the shopping center had a mortgage of $150,000, which you assumed, that mortgage balance would be treated as if you received cash of $150,000—that is, it would be taxable. If both properties have mortgages, only the net difference between the two mortgage balances would be considered cash. (The party assuming the higher mortgage would be treated as if it received cash in the amount of the net difference.)

Deferred Like-kind Exchanges It is possible to prearrange a nontaxable exchange. You transfer your apartment building to Alice, specifying in the contract that she is to purchase a property of your choosing and transfer it to you. This will be considered a nontaxable exchange if the property you want is identified within 45 days and is received within 180 days or the due date for filing the tax return for that year.

Multiparty Exchanges This will work also: Archie transfers property to Betty. Betty transfers property to Charlene, and Charlene transfers property to Archie.

More Rules on Like-kind Exchanges There are more hoops to jump through. For instance, if you exchange property with a related property (your relative, your corporation, etc.), the rules are complex. Inasmuch as experiencing the IRS disallowing your exchange and facing a large tax bill would be a nightmare, you should hire a knowledgeable tax professional to guide you through the transaction.

Income from Renting All or Part of Your Residence(s)

There are several situations that fit this description, and each is impacted by a different set of rules.

Converting Your Residence to Rental Property

The day your residence is empty and you offer it for rent (as in advertising it) is the day you start recording expenses that can be deducted from the rental income, even if you do not find a suitable tenant for several weeks.

If you have never rented the house before or taken a depreciation deduction (as for office-in-home), depreciation computations start for the month in which you offered the residence for rent. Your basis is your original cost of the house, plus the acquisition costs (fees, etc. that are on your original buyer's closing statement) and later additions (pool, fence, added rooms, etc.).

Tax Benefits You Lose When You Convert Your Residence to Rental

First disadvantage: You lose the tax break of deferring tax on the gain when you sell your residence. Because the building is now rental property, if you sell it later, you will have a capital gain tax to pay. (See Chapter 7.)

Second disadvantage: If you have owned your residence for many years, your basis on which you compute the depreciation will be very low, so your resulting deduction of depreciation expense will be very low.

EXPERT ADVICE

Sell your residence, even if you have to accept something less than the price you expected. Buy another house to use as rental property with the proceeds. If you are planning to buy or build another residence (including a boat or vehicle with living accommodations) within two years, or if you are over 55 and eligible, you will defer or escape from capital gains tax on sale of your residence.

Then, use the proceeds to buy another house to offer for rental. Now, your basis for depreciation will be based on today's market values, which should mean much higher depreciation deductions.

Example: *You bought your residence 30 years ago for $25,000. Today, you can sell it, quickly, for $150,000, or you can convert it to rental property and sell it three years later for $150,000. (It didn't appreciate because of wear and tear by tenants.)*

EXPERT ADVICE *(CONTINUED)*

Convert to rental:

Basis for depreciation (assuming land was worth
$5,000 when you bought the property) is $20,000

Annual depreciation deduction ($20,000 ÷ 27.5) $727

Sale of property in three years:

Sale price	$150,000
Subtract basis (cost minus depreciation)	22,819
Gain on which you pay tax	127,181
Tax at 20%	$ 25,436

Sell residence and buy another property to rent:

Sale of property	$150,000
Basis	25,000
Gain	125,000
Tax you do not need to pay	$ 25,000

Basis of new rental property is $150,000
(Land is $30,000)

Annual depreciation: $120,000 ÷ 27.5 years = $ 4,364

Which is more appealing?

An annual depreciation deduction of $727 or $4,364?

A tax of $25,436 or one of 0.00?

Rent Your Residence and Avoid the Pitfalls If your intent is to sell your residence, but circumstances make that impossible, you can rent it for a short period and still claim a deferral of gain when you sell it.

Duplex—And You Live in One Unit

This situation is unusual in tax law: it's logical and straightforward. If each unit in the duplex is the same size, you divide every expense 50-50. If one unit is larger than the other, determine a ratio based on the square feet of living space, or on some other logical measure (e.g., your apartment in the attic is not as desirable as the one on the first floor, so make an adjustment in the ratio).

Divide all of the expenses according to the ratio. Those that are allocated to the rented unit are deducted from the rental income. Those that are allocated to your unit are personal expenses, but remember that your share of the mortgage interest and real estate taxes can be deducted as itemized deductions on Schedule A. (See Chapter 10.)

As for depreciation, divide the basis of the improvements (building, etc.) between the two units, based on the same ratio as the expenses. Compute the depreciation on the rented half only and deduct it from the rental income, as for any rental property. Your half is never depreciated and it qualifies for the tax-free gain from the sale of a principal residence sale.

Office Space in Your Home

If you use part of your home as an office for your business, you may have a tax deduction.

What Makes Your Home Office Deductible To be able to deduct the cost of the home office, that office must be your *principal place of business* and the office space must be used exclusively for the business. (Space that you use for storing inventory that belongs to you also qualifies.) Of course, it would qualify if you spend nearly all of your working time there, as for a free-lance computer programmer or writer. It also qualifies if there is no other fixed business location from which to perform management and administrative activities (and you conduct these activities in your home office). *Note: Prior to 1997, the definition of "principal place of business" was far more limiting.*

Exception for day care: If you use the business space for a day-care operation, you do not have to meet the requirement that the space be used exclusively for business. You do, however, have to allocate expenses to the business use of your home not only by area used but by the time the area is used.

Use of Office Space in Your Home for Your Job The same rules as for your own business apply. However, as an employee, you can deduct these expenses only as a "miscellaneous deduction" on Schedule A. That means it is subject to the 2 percent floor, so the deduction may be of no benefit. (See Chapter 10.)

Home Office, the Computation Details If you claim this deduction, use Form 8829 to make the computations.

Use of Office Space in Your Home for Your Investment Activities Congress gives, and Congress takes away, and this is a tax deduction our lawmakers took away. You cannot deduct the expenses of a home office that you use for your investing, as in stocks, bonds, or mutual funds. Neither can you deduct it if you use it for investing in rental property, unless your real estate meets the qualifications of being treated as a business. (See the discussion of passive real estate income earlier in this chapter.)

Should You Bother Taking a Home Office Deduction? When you allocate expenses between your residence and your office, remember that mortgage interest and taxes are fully deductible as itemized deductions anyway. Do the other expenses result in a large enough deduction to be worth the hassle? As explained later in this chapter, the deduction of depreciation of your home will result in immediate capital gain tax when you sell your home (for the business portion). Work out the numbers both ways and make a decision.

If you rent your residence, then you have nothing to lose and a tax deduction to gain if you deduct part of the rent you pay for your home office (assuming it meets the requirements).

CAUTION

If your office space would qualify for the home office deduction, but you do not take it, the IRS could take the position that part of your home was a business location and, therefore, capital gains taxes would be due on the sale of that part. Therefore, if you forgo this deduction, disqualify your office space by using it for personal purposes for a significant amount of time during the year. (Suggestions: Kid's homework, personal letters, personal finance activities, and hobbies.)

If you have an office in your home, the mechanics of determining what part of your expenses are deductible, and computing depreciation is similar to allocating expenses of the duplex, described earlier. However, the IRS insists that you make the computations on Form 8829. Unfortunately, the IRS has to design the form to fit everyone who might fill it out. (For instance, the "excess mortgage interest" line is there for those who have more than $1,000,000 of home acquisition mortgage debt or more than $100,000 of home equity mortgage debt. Most of us do not fall into that category, but the line has to be there for those who do.) The result is a complex form with instructions to match, so this is another argument for using tax preparation software or the services of a professional—after you have read about the basics.

Rental of Vacation Home

That vacation home you own at the seashore or in the mountains or anywhere sits empty much of the time. Why not earn some extra cash by renting it, or better yet, use it to generate a loss that you may be able to deduct (if you meet the qualifications for a deduction of up to $25,000 or have passive income). The basic rule is that, if the numbers generate a rental loss when you rent out your cottage, you can use that loss if you use the cottage personally for no more than whichever is the greater number of days:

- 10 percent of the total number of days the property is rented; or
- 14 days.

CAUTION

When you count days of personal use, count the days the cottage is used by other members of your family, regardless of any rent they may have paid you. For this rule, family members are spouse, brothers and sisters (whole or half-blood), ancestors, and lineal descendants. (Note the difference between renting a vacation home to your sister and renting her an apartment or house as her principal residence [covered early in this chapter].)

You have three alternatives:

Escape Hatch If you like to avoid intricate computations and having to keep a record of where you were and what you did, rent the cottage to others for a total of less than 15 days. Unbelievably, you do not report the money the tenants pay you as income. The downside is that you cannot deduct any of the expenses of your vacation home if you use this escape hatch.

Turn the Cottage into a Strictly Rental Property To do that, you cannot use it personally. Stay away from it except to do maintenance on it (*work full time* on each maintenance day) or to show the property to prospective tenants, collect rent, and do other management activities.

Two rules are a variation of the full-time rental approach: First, if you rent it for 12 months or more that begin or end in a year, the limitations on rental expenses do not apply. Second, if you rent it for any period and sell (or exchange it) at the end of the period, the limitations do not apply.

Disregard the 14-day/10 Percent Rule If you go this route, you can deduct rental expenses only up to the amount of rental income. You cannot deduct additional expenses to create a rental loss, although you can carry them forward to another year in which you might have more rental income.

Live Within the 14-day/10 Percent Rule Keep records to prove what few days you used the cottage and what days were devoted to maintenance, so you can end up with a deductible loss to use on your tax return.

Gain or Loss When You Sell Your *Principal Residence*

During the year 1997, we have two rules for computing the tax on the sale of your principal residence. (If you closed on your sale before May 7, 1997, you may have been had! But there is a way out.)

Old Rules (But They Still Affect the New Rules)

If you sold your home before May 7, 1997, you can defer $125,000 of the gain if you reinvest the proceeds of the sale into another home. The key word here is "defer," as in "tax is deferred, not canceled." The mechanics of deferring the gain reduce the basis of each house you owned, so that your current house has a basis that is much lower than the price you paid for it.

Example:

In 1975 you bought your first home for	$ 25,000
In 1985 you sold your first home for	100,000
Gain on which tax is deferred	$ 75,000
In 1985 you bought a replacement home for	$ 80,000
Deduct gain (tax deferred) on first home	75,000
Basis of this replacement home	$ 5,000

In 1993, when you are 47 years old, you chuck this modern lifestyle, sell your home, move to a tropical island, and live in a tent under a palm tree.

You sell your home that you purchased in 1985 for	$200,000
Subtract basis of home (from above)	5,000
Gain (taxable)	$195,000
Capital gain tax at 28 percent	$ 54,000

That gain on the sale of the replacement home is taxable because you did not reinvest the proceeds of the sale in another home. Had you reinvested even part of the proceeds, only part of the $195,000 gain would be taxable.

If you were age 55 or older when you sold the replacement residence, you can elect to take advantage of the once-a-lifetime exclusion of $125,000 of gain when you sell your home. In the example, that would lower your taxable gain to $75,000.

New Rules

New rules can result in tax-free sale of your home.

If you sell your *principal residence* after May 6, 1997, you can exclude $500,000 of gain on the house if you file a joint return. (The number is $250,000 for single and separate returns.) No longer is there a requirement that you reinvest the proceeds. However, you can make such a tax-free sale of your home only once every two years, and you must have lived in the house for a combined period of two years out of the last five years.

Because not all gain but only the first $500,000 (or $250,000) of it escapes tax, you will still need to compute your gain. So, you will need old records to determine your basis under the old rules. If, in our example above, you sold the replacement home in June 1997 for $600,000 (perhaps the land between your home and the ocean washed away in a hurricane, so you are now on waterfront property), the taxable gain computation would look like this:

Sale of home	$600,000
Basis of home	5,000
Total gain	595,000
Gain excluded from tax	500,000
Taxable gain	95,000
Capital gain tax at 28%	$ 26,600

More Rules and Comments

If you do manually complete your own tax forms, the instructions for the appropriate form should lead you through the computations. Form 2119 and its instructions for 1996 was comprehensive and would serve to determine the basis of your residence under the old rules. How the IRS will handle the reporting of gain under both the old rules and the new rules for 1997 is, at this writing, unknown.

Highlights of Old Rules If a couple wanted to take advantage of the exclusion of $125,000 if one of them is age 55 or over, they cannot do so if one of the spouses has already used the once-a-lifetime allowance when single or married to someone else. (Such a spouse is called a "tainted spouse" in tax jargon. If someone tells you that you are "tainted," tell them that it "ain't so after May 6, 1997.")

Our example used a history of only two residences, to keep it simple. It was possible to change residences every two years and keep deferring the taxable gain on several homes.

If you ever used part of your residence for business purposes (e.g., home office), the total of depreciation that you claimed in all years reduces the basis of the property. If you used your home for business in the year you sold the property, you paid tax (it was not deferred) on the gain allocated to the business portion of your home. If no part of your home was used for business in the year of sale, the total accumulated depreciation from previous years still reduced your basis, but all of the gain was considered gain on your residence and therefore may be deferred—if the other conditions were met.

Highlights of New Rules You can avail yourself of the exclusion of tax on gain only once every two years. Also, you must have owned and used the property as your principal residence for a combined period of two years out of the previous five years.

Depreciation deducted after June 6, 1997, for any business use of the home will generate taxable gain when the house is sold, even if there is no business use in the year of sale.

Comments Applicable to Both Rules When computing the basis of a residence, remember to add the cost of improvements you made to the property. (The instructions for Form 2119 contain a extensive check list. It will prod your memory, but it is better to have invoices and receipts.)

The deferral or exclusion of tax on sale of a principal residence does *not* apply to a vacation or second home.

EXPERT ADVICE

Did you sell your residence before May 7, 1997, did not replace it, and are not eligible for the over-55 exclusion of $125,000 gain? Are you looking forward to paying a large capital gain tax? Do this:

Spend at least as much as the selling price of your home for a new residence. Keep it, and use it as your principal residence for two years, then sell it. Now you can exclude $500,000 of gain (on a joint return).

Did you have travel plans? Note that the IRS says your principal residence is the one you live in most of the time. It does not say all of the time.

Consider using the sale proceeds to buy and travel in an RV or boat. They can qualify as a principal residence, thereby sheltering your gain on the home sale, if you keep the RV or boat for two years. Yes, they do lose value over time, but that loss of value may be far less than the capital gain tax you will pay if you take no action, particularly if you purchase a "pre-owned" RV or boat.

Royalty Income

Royalty income consists of money (usually) others pay to you for extraction from or use of your property. There are two basic types of this income: That which comes from extraction of natural resources (including timber) and that which comes from intangible property (patents, copyrights, etc.).

Royalty Income from the Extraction/Cutting of Resources

If you have land with coal in it and you allow a coal company to mine it, you obviously would expect compensation, which would be a royalty. Usually, it takes the form of so much per ton mined, per acre of timber cut, or some other measurement of extraction.

Usually, the royalty is ordinary income, and from it you can deduct expenses such as legal fees, telephone calls, postage, automobile use, and other expenses incurred in contracting for and collecting royalties.

Also, you can deduct depletion, which is similar to depreciation. Depletion is a deduction you are allowed to take to reflect the fact that the resource that is being mined or cut is being used up. As a step toward making our tax system as complicated as possible, Congress has authorized two methods of computing depletion.

Cost Depletion

This most closely resembles depreciation. Assume you own land with a basis of $100,000, under which experts estimate there are 1,000,000 tons of coal. During the year, a coal company mines 200,000 tons of coal, on which the company pays you a royalty of one dollar per ton.

During this year, the coal company has extracted 200,000 ÷ 1,000,000, or 20 percent of the total coal under your land. Your depletion deduction is therefore 20 percent of the basis of your land (20% × $100,000) or $20,000.

Percentage Depletion

Instead of making the calculations and having to guess at the in-ground reserves of a resource, you can take a percentage of the gross royalty income as a depletion deduction. For instance, for coal the percentage is 10 percent. So, in the above situation, percentage depletion is 10 percent of $200,000, or $20,000.

Amazingly, you can deduct more percentage depletion than the basis of your land.

But there are other limitations on seemingly endless deduction: You cannot deduct more than 50 percent of the "taxable income from the property." That is defined as the gross royalty less all of the deductible expenses except depletion. (The percentage is 100 for oil and gas properties.)

You cannot use percentage depletion for timber, soil, sod, dirt, water, mosses, and minerals from sea water or the air.

Another amazing rule is that you can deduct either cost depletion or percentage depletion each year resources are extracted—it's your choice. The amount of either type of depletion deduction must be subtracted from the basis of the land. When the basis gets down to zero, that's the end of cost depletion. But you can deduct percentage depletion as long as someone pays you royalties.

This royalty income is reported on Schedule E. Also, note that this income, most probably, is passive income or loss to you.

Royalty Income from Copyrights, Patents, and Other Intangibles

If you are a writer or inventor, you will, we hope, receive royalties from those who publish or produce and market your book or gadget. This "royalty" income is really a form of compensation to you for the personal labor you performed. It is therefore more in the nature of a small business income, and that is how the IRS wants you to report it—on a Schedule C. That's not all bad, for it enables you to deduct expenses just as can any business, including a home office.

There is no deduction for depreciation or depletion of the copyright or invention if you are the creator of the intangible. (Your principal investment was your time, so you have no basis for depreciation.)

Is the net income from this activity subject to Social Security tax? The rule is this: If you write one book, perhaps as an adjunct to your profession, or just for the enjoyment of recording your thoughts, any resulting royalty income is not subject to Social Security tax. However, if you write as a career, producing several books or a stream of magazine articles, then your activities are viewed as a major income-producing activity, and you are supposed to pay Social Security tax on your net income from your writing.

If, perchance, you have purchased an interest in a copyright or invention, then you probably have passive investment, and you report that on Schedule E. Unless you acquired these intangible assets as part of a purchase of business, you cannot amortize their costs. ("Amortization" is similar to depreciation but refers to the partial annual deduction of the cost of an intangible asset.)

Retirement and Other Withdrawals from Retirement Funds

9

- Those who are approaching retirement
- Those who are retired
- Those who are totally disabled
- Those who need cash for education or buying their first home
- Those who are changing jobs
- Those who plan ahead

THIS CHAPTER INCLUDES

- When and how you can take money out of a retirement plan
- How to take cash out of your IRA for education
- How much you can take out of your IRA to help buy your first home
- How to avoid penalties when you make rollovers to or between IRAs
- How to protect your Social Security benefits
- When you can work part time

FAST FORWARD

Taking Money Out of Your Retirement Plan ➤ pp. 139–144

- You can take funds out of your retirement plan, either on a monthly schedule or in a lump sum, once you reach age 59½. You can take it out earlier under specific circumstances: early retirement, medical expenses, college education expenses, and first-time home buyer. (Starting in 1998 for the last two circumstances.)
- You can rollover from retirement plan to retirement plan, but be careful that the withholding tax rules don't snag you.
- Special averaging tax rules can apply to lump sum distributions, depending on your age.

Social Security ➤ pp. 145–148

- Social Security benefits can be blown away if you work too hard. Avoid paying money for the privilege of working.

Retirement income can come from many sources: Your employer's retirement plan; your tax-sheltered savings, such as an IRA; your after-tax savings; various investments, including stocks, bonds, and real estate; value of your residence; value of your business; Social Security benefits; and the continuation of some level of employment as part of your retirement. The effect of taxation rules and of the interaction of the various forms of retirement on your tax liability can be mind-boggling. This discussion of basic concepts, rules, and areas where penalties may "getcha" should get you through the maze.

Do not overlook other help that may be available. Your employer, if the company is large, should have a benefits department that can explain choices of how to withdraw benefits from your employer's retirement plan. If you work for a small company, there should be a benefit plan consultant in the picture who can help you. Armed with this advice that is free, run it by your tax professional, who should know your individual situation, for help in making any elections as to withdrawals.

Taking Money Out of Your Retirement Plan

General Rules About Plan Distributions

The magic age is 59½. If you are past that, you may start withdrawing cash from your retirement. As you withdraw the money, you pay income tax on it. That's because you did not pay tax on the money that went into the plan or on the earnings of the investments in the plan. (However, that is not true with the Roth IRA, discussed later.)

Another number, with less magic involved, is age 70½. This is the age at which most of us have to start taking withdrawals from the plan and paying tax on the withdrawals whether we need the cash or not.

Exceptions to the Age 59½ Rule

Rollover Exception

A rollover is the act of moving your money in an employer's retirement plan to another employer's plan, or from an employer's plan to an IRA, or between IRAs. If you roll over the balance in your retirement account to another account, there is no penalty for being too young, for you have actually tapped into your retirement plan for other purposes. The need for a rollover often occurs because you are changing jobs, your employer is discontinuing its retirement plan, or, in the case of IRAs, you think the earnings will be higher in a different IRA.

The rollover can be from employer plan to employer plan or employer plan to your IRA. You can roll over from an IRA to an employer plan only the funds in the IRA that came from an employer plan. (This is useful if you leave one job and do not find another one for several months.) You can also roll over from one IRA to another IRA, and those funds can come from your own contributions.

Don't Let the IRS Borrow Your Money and Then Penalize You There was a time when you could take a lump sum out of an IRA or an employer's plan when you switched jobs and keep the cash in your pocket (or regular bank account) for 60 days before you rolled it over to another IRA. You can still do that, but it will cost you, because now the IRS will make the custodian of the plan you take the money from withhold 20 percent of the lump sum and send it off to the IRS. Then, at the end of the 60-day period, to avoid a large withdrawal penalty, you have to put 100 percent of that money into another plan or IRA, but you have only 80 percent of your IRA funds left. So, you'll have to dig into your emergency savings for or borrow the 20 percent that the IRS took, or pay a penalty.

Example: You have $50,000 in your retirement account at your employer, Sinking Corporation, when you decide to seek other employment. You ask for the $50,000 in your account, but Sinking Corporation pays you only $40,000. It sends the other $10,000 off to the IRS. Thirty days later you find a new job at Expanding Corporation, which has a retirement plan that accepts rollovers. You write a check to the new pension plan for the $40,000 you have, but you have to arrange a second mortgage on your house in order to borrow the other $10,000, and that's expensive.

If you don't put that $10,000 in the new retirement plan, the $10,000 is a "premature distribution." The IRS will want you to pay income tax on that $10,000 plus a penalty of $1,000 (10 percent of the premature distribution).

You will get your $10,000 back from the IRS if you claim it as withheld tax on your tax return for the year, and that should result in a refund. However, that will be many months away.

What should you have done? You could have left the funds in Sinking Corporation's pension plan until you found the new job and then have had the administrator at Sinking transfer the funds to Expanding. If, despite the safeguards that the federal pension laws impose, you want to get your money out of Sinking's plan right away, have the administrator send the funds directly to an IRA you set up at your bank or some financial institution. (Set up a separate IRA for this purpose so that it is easy to identify the funds that came from Sinking's plan.) After you start work at Expanding, have the bank roll over the IRA funds to Expanding's retirement plan.

Death Exception

This is not the recommended way to obtain your retirement benefits early, but if you should die early, your heirs become entitled to the funds.

Disability Exception

If you are totally disabled, you can withdraw retirement funds at any age.

Separation from Service After Age 55

You can withdraw funds a little early if you quit or are terminated (as in "downsized"). Note that this can be a lump sum withdrawal, whereas the next rule must be a series of payments.

Withdrawals Made by a Series of Equal Payments

At any age, if you leave your job, you can start withdrawing from your retirement plan if the withdrawal consists of a series of equal payments made at least annually. The payments must be small enough to last for your life expectancy or the life expectancy of the joint lives of you and your beneficiary.

Some Medical Expense Exceptions

You can withdraw funds from your IRA at any age to cover the part of your medical expense that is greater than 7.5 percent of your adjusted gross income.

Also, you can withdraw funds from an IRA to pay medical insurance premiums if you have received unemployment compensation for at least 12 weeks (or could have except for being self-employed).

"First-time Homebuyer" Expense Exception

This new law is effective for 1998 and beyond.

You can withdraw funds from your IRA, at any age and without penalty, if you use them within 120 days to pay the costs of acquiring a residence. These costs are defined as the cost of acquiring, constructing, or reconstructing a residence, and they also include any usual or reasonable settlement, financing, or other closing costs.

The maximum you can withdraw is $10,000, and you cannot withdraw more than that during your lifetime. As I write this, it is not clear whether the $10,000 exclusion is per individual or per married couple.

A "first-time home buyer" is someone who has not owned a residence in the two-year period ending on the date he or she buys a home. If a married couple buy a home, they both must qualify under this rule.

Higher Education Expense Exception

Starting in 1998, you can withdraw funds from an IRA to pay for college-level undergraduate and post-graduate education for you, your spouse, child (yours or your spouse's), or grandchild.

CAUTION

When planning your cash flow, remember that withdrawals from IRAs, including those for medical expense, home-buying expense, and education expense, are subject to income tax. These new rules avoid the 10 percent penalty for early withdrawal.

Exception: You can also withdraw funds for the home-buying expense and educational expense purposes from the new Roth IRA, and those funds would not be taxable because you paid tax on them when you contributed to the Roth IRA.

Form to File

If you didn't follow these rules, you are probably liable for a 10 percent penalty (10 percent of the amount you withdrew), and you compute the penalty on Form 5329. Also, if you made a withdrawal but are eligible for one of the above exceptions, you can tell that to the IRS on the same form.

Withdrawals Starting At Age 70½ Rule

Withdrawals must start by April 1 of the year after you reach age 70½. There is an exception: If you are still working, the date is April 1 of the year after you retire. The amount of the payments have to be enough to withdraw all of the funds in the plan over your life expectancy or over the joint life expectancy of you and your beneficiary.

Lump Sum Payments from Retirement Plans

Some lump sum distributions from retirement plans are eligible for special tax breaks. To be eligible for treatment as a lump sum under income tax rules, the lump sum has to be the entire balance of your account in an employer's retirement plan. It has to be paid to you or your beneficiary for one of the following reasons:

- You have been separated from your employment. (Self-employed people do not qualify for this one.)
- You have reached age 59½.
- You have died.
- You are self-employed and have become disabled.
- You have not previously rolled over a distribution from this plan to another plan or an IRA.

Lump sum payments to you are taxed in one of the following ways:

Report All of the Lump Sum as Income in the Year You Receive It

This will not be attractive for most people, as it would push the recipient into a much higher tax bracket.

Five-year Averaging

This splits the lump sum payment into five equal parts, computes the tax on each part, and then multiplies the resulting tax by five to compute the total tax on the distribution. The tax rate that applies is that of a single taxpayer, modified by the complex computation for a "minimum distribution allowance." Rather than worry with that, just use the tax rates in the instructions to Form 4972 (which incorporate that allowance), or better, let your tax software figure out the tax.

You must have been in the retirement plan for five years to use this averaging.

CAUTION

This five-year averaging provision of the tax is scheduled to expire at the end of 1999. You may find it advantageous to plan for a lump sum payment prior to that time.

Ten-year Averaging

To qualify for this provision, you must have been born before 1936. If you were a participant in the employer's plan before 1974, some of the lump sum payment will be eligible for capital-gain treatment. How much? Your employer's plan administrator should have computed that and put the number in Box 3 of the 1099-R you receive. You can then compute the tax on that capital gain at 20 percent or, if it works out to result in less tax, include it in the lump sum for which you compute the tax by 10-year averaging. The computation computes the tax on one-tenth of the lump sum to be taxed and then multiples that result by 10, and the computation is based on 1986 tax rates.

How do you tell if you are better off to report the capital gain as taxed at 20 percent? Generally, if the lump sum is larger than $137,100, you should work out the computation both ways. If the lump sum is smaller, forgo the capital gain option.

Again, the computation can be done on Form 4972, and you can find the tax rates in the instructions for the form—or use tax software.

Employer's Securities That Are Included in a Lump Sum Distribution

If the lump sum distribution to you includes stocks and/or bonds issued by the employer, the figure you pay tax on is the cost to the plan when the securities were purchased by the plan. Any appreciation in the value of the stock since is called "net unrealized appreciation" and is often abbreviated to "NUA." That number appears in Box 6 of the 1099-R you receive, and it does not need to be included in taxable income until you sell the stock. You can, however, elect to have it included in income for the year you receive the securities in the lump sum. (You might so elect if you expect to be in a higher tax bracket later.) Your choice affects your basis (and how much taxable gain you will have later) as follows.

If you do not elect immediate taxation, your basis of the security is its original cost to the retirement plan. If you do elect immediate taxation, your basis is the original cost plus the amount on which you are taxed now.

If your employer's securities are worth less than employer's cost, their basis is the fair market value on the date they were distributed, and that is also the amount included in the taxable distribution total.

Social Security

For middle- and high-income retirees, Social Security is just as taxable as is most all income. (The government gives, and the government takes back.) A quick but incomplete test is this: Compute your adjusted gross income (page one of Form 1040 makes a handy vehicle for this), but do not include any Social Security benefits in that figure. Add tax-exempt income. If the total exceeds a "base amount," at least part of your Social Security benefits are taxable. The base amount is as follows:

Married, filing joint return	$32,000
Married, filing separate who lives with his or her spouse for at least part of the year	0
All others	$25,000

This quick test will not be accurate if you have excluded foreign income and housing costs, savings bond proceeds for education expense, employer-provided adoption assistance, and/or income from sources within U.S. possessions and Puerto Rico.

How Much of Your Social Security Will Be Taxable?

The taxable portion of your Social Security benefit (or benefits, on a joint return) may be none up to 85 percent. Exactly how much is a complex calculation, so there are no easy formulas. If your affairs do not include any of the items in the previous paragraph, you can probably use the worksheet in the IRS-published instructions to Form 1040. If you do have any of those items in your financial picture, you will have to use the worksheets in IRS Publication 915. It's free at 1-800-829-3676. (If you are receiving Social Security benefits and are a participant in an employer's retirement plan and you make nontaxable IRA contributions, you will also need the special rules in that IRS publication.)

Tax on Part-time Employment After You Retire

Very few retired people have what they consider enough income. There always seem to be incentives to pick up a part-time job to pay for some extra travel or other activities. However, if you are under age 70, tread carefully. Your Social Security benefits will decrease if you earn too much money from your employment. In addition, your wages will increase your taxable income, possibly making more of your Social Security benefits taxable. Here are the basic rules, using 1997 figures:

- If you are age 62, 63, or 64, your benefit will decrease $1 for every $2 of wages over $8,640 per year.
- If you are age 65 through 69, your benefit will decrease $1 for every $3 of wages over $13,500 per year.

In certain circumstances, it is possible for someone to suffer a net loss of cash, after the benefit reduction and increased taxes, if they earn more than the above figures. What to do? If you are offered work that will generate wages or salary above the $8,640 or $13,500 annual amounts, work out your tax return for the current year with and without that increase. As mentioned above, the calculations can be complex, so tax preparation software would be helpful. Failing that, it may save you a lot of working-for-nothing hours to engage a tax preparer to work the numbers for you.

There is another alternative if you can perform your part-time work as a self-employed individual. Set up your business as an S corporation (see Chapter 5), pay yourself only a reasonable salary, and let the additional profits accumulate in the corporation. Then, withdraw those profits from the S corporation as distributions, which are not considered wages for Social Security purposes.

Example: Ernest, who is a retired framing contractor, is 66 years old and wants to stay busy. He projects that by spending 500 hours as a remodeling contractor, he can earn $20,000. To stay busy, he will do the work himself, but he could hire semi-skilled labor to do the work at $15 per hour.

He applies for and receives from his state a corporate charter for Ideal Remodeling, Inc. Then he sends off Form 2553 to the IRS to elect S corporation status for Ideal. Then, as the work progresses, Ideal pays him $15 per hour for his 500 hours of manual labor plus another $1,000 for his administrative duties. Ideal Remodeling's year-end tax return looks like this:

Total contract sales		$20,000
Subtract:		
Wages paid ($15 × 500 hours)	$7,500	
Administrative salary paid	1,000	
Total expenses		8,500
Net income of corporation		$11,500

The net income of the corporation, because it is an S corporation, is included on Ernest's Form 1040, as are the wages and salary he received. (As the president of Ideal Remodeling, Inc., Ernest must generate a W-2 for himself, showing total wages and salaries of $8,500.)

Ernest's tax return reports only $8,500 on the "wages, salaries and tips" line of his Form 1040. The $11,500 of net income from the corporation goes on Ernest's Schedule E as "income from an S corporation." The result is that his earnings for Social Security purposes are only $8,500, far below the loss-of-benefit threshold of $13,500. The $11,500 is in the corporation's bank account, but as the sole director of the corporation, Ernest is free to declare a tax-free distribution of cash to himself any time he wishes.

This may sound like an expensive process, but it need not be. You don't need a silk-stocking law firm to set up a simple one-stockholder corporation. The incorporation services that advertise in business and other periodicals are adequate for your needs. Also, don't be talked into incorporating in Delaware or Nevada. It's not necessary for this simple operation.

Conclusion

There are several tax alternatives in how you take funds from your retirement account. Consider them carefully and do some computations. The best way to do them is by working out the probable tax return for each alternative. (Again, an argument for tax preparation software.) Plan your tax and working life so that, if possible, your Social Security benefits don't disappear.

10

Personal Expenses You Can Deduct (Itemized Deductions)

- Everyone (Even if they usually claim the standard deduction, they need to assure themselves that they do not have more in itemized deductions.)

THIS CHAPTER INCLUDES

- Deductible medical expense (you have to be real sick)

- Taxes you can still deduct

- Interest expense (not much without a mortgage)

- Charitable contributions—make sure they're deductions

- Casualty loss deduction—a little help from the government

- How to make more of the tax preparation fee deductible

- Deductible investment expenses

FAST FORWARD

Medical Expense ➤ *pp. 151–154*

- Medical expenses are deductible only if they total more than 7.5 percent of adjusted gross income, and then only the expenses above that amount are deductible. Unless you have large medical expense or very low income, it's not worth searching records and listing these expenses.

Other Itemized Deductions ➤ *pp. 154–165*

- The list of deductible taxes has been much reduced over the years. All that is left are some income taxes, real estate taxes, and personal property taxes.
- Some interest expense is deductible, but unless it's mortgage interest or interest on money borrowed for buying investments, it probably isn't a deduction.
- Charitable contributions are deductible if you follow the rules as to how much and obtain the right documents.
- Casualty losses are deductible, but only those that are in excess of 10 percent of your adjusted gross income.
- This is where you deduct the unreimbursed employee business expense we discussed in Chapter 4.
- And there are some miscellaneous deductions: tax preparation, investment expenses, and a few others.

Since almost the inception of the federal income tax, the rules have allowed a deduction for various personal expenses; and the rules and the expenses allowed have changed from time to time. In this chapter we will ignore the theories as to why Congress has selected these expenses as deductions and look at how best to use the rules for your benefit. These expenses are claimed on Schedule A of Form 1040.

Medical Expense

You can deduct medical expenses that exceed 7.5 percent of your adjusted gross income, so compute that AGI (see Chapter 11) before you continue in this section.

Example: Your adjusted gross income is $50,000. 7.5 percent of that is $3,750. If you have less than that in medical expense, you have no deduction for medical expense.

The rules generally describe medical expenses as amounts paid for:

- Diagnosis, mitigation, treatment, and prevention of disease, or for the purpose of affecting any structure or function of the body.
- Nursing services.
- Eyeglasses, artificial teeth or limbs, hearing aids, and similar items.
- Prescription drugs and insulin. (Over-the-counter drugs are not eligible for deduction.)

Hospitalization Expense

The expense of a stay in a hospital or similar institution, including room and board, is deductible if the patient is there primarily for medical reasons. Whether that is so depends on the patient's condition, not on the type of institution.

Example: Tuition, meals, and lodging for a physically or mentally handicapped student at a special school are deductible. Nursing home expenses are deductible if the individual is there principally for medical reasons.

Long-term Care Facilities

Long-term care, including necessary diagnostic, preventive, therapeutic, curing, treating, mitigating, and rehabilitative services, as well as maintenance and personal care services required by a chronically ill individual, are deductible starting in 1997. The personal care services must be provided under a plan prescribed by a licensed health care practitioner.

Accident and Health Insurance

To be deductible, the insurance policy must cover only medical care as outlined in the previous points.

- Check your automobile and boat insurance. The part of the premium for medical coverage is deductible accident and health insurance, provided it is separately stated and reasonable.

- Are you 65 or over and covered by Medicare insurance? The supplementary *voluntary* Part B insurance qualifies for this deduction, as does *voluntary* payment of Part A premiums by the few people who are not eligible for automatic Part A coverage. Remember to include the cost of any supplemental medical insurance you may pay for.

- Long-term care insurance premiums are deductible starting in 1997, within annual limits, depending upon your age at the end of the year:

Age 40 or less	$ 200
Age 41 through 50	$ 375
Age 51 through 60	$ 750
Age 61 through 70	$2,000
Over age 70	$2,500

Expenditures for Medical Equipment or Improvements

If the expenditure, such as for a swimming pool or elevator, has the primary purpose of being for the medical care of the resident, it is deductible. Actually, the improvement may be only partly deductible if it increases the value of the residence.

Example: Sheila has a medical condition that requires she swim extensively. She has a swimming pool and enclosure built behind her $100,000 home at a cost of

$20,000. Because the pool raises the market value of her home to $108,000, she can deduct only $12,000 ($108,000 minus the $8,000 increase in the value of her home) as medical expense.

If the medically necessary equipment is portable or removable (for example, a room air conditioner), there is no increase in the value of the property, so the full cost should be deductible.

CAUTION

The IRS is prone to question large expenditures for swimming pools and other enhancements that you might claim as medical expense. Lay your groundwork with statements from health professionals, medical journal articles, and any other documentation that might prove the medical purpose of the improvement.

Transportation and Travel as a Deductible Medical Expense

Trips to the doctor, hospital, and other medical facilities are deductible. If you use your automobile, total up the gas, parking fees, and tolls for the trips, or you can compute the mileage at 10 cents per mile and add the parking fees and tolls. If you must travel or stay out of town for medical care, you can deduct the cost of lodging up to a limit of $50 per day. Meals are not deductible, and the trip must be for medical care, not for pleasure or vacation.

Payment and Insurance Reimbursement

Take the medical care deduction in the year in which you pay it, even if the bill is for care in a previous year. (Paying in advance for next year's care usually will not work, but see the section above on long-term care.) Do not deduct expenses for which you received insurance reimbursement.

If you deducted expenses in one year and received reimbursement in the next year, you may have income in the year of recovery, as this example illustrates.

Example:

Edna's medical expense last year was		$4,000
Her adjusted gross income was	$50,000	
7.5 percent of her adjusted gross income was		3,750
Her deductible medical expense was		$ 250

This year, her insurance company sends her a check for $1,000 as reimbursement for last year's medical expense. However, because she was able to use only $250 of that medical expense as a tax deduction, only $250 of that $1,000 check is income to her. She reports it as income on this year's tax return, on the "other income" line.

Where to Deduct

Medical expenses are deducted on Schedule A, which incorporates the subtraction of the 7.5 percent of gross income.

Taxes You Can Deduct as Itemized Deductions

Deductible taxes can be separated into three categories:

1. Taxes that are deductible just because they are taxes.
2. Taxes that can be deducted only if they represent a business or, in some cases, an investment expense.
3. Taxes that become part of the cost or basis of property.

Taxes That Are Deductible as Taxes

These include:

State and Local Income Taxes

On the face of it, this computation is simple. You just add together the state and local income taxes that have been withheld from your salary and the checks you have sent off to the state or local treasurer. But no tax rule can be that simple.

Consider state income tax: If you overpay (by check or withholding) your state tax, you will receive a refund—and a Form 1099 telling the IRS that you received the refund. So, you have to report the refund as income on page one of Form 1040. If you allowed the refund to be applied to your estimated tax, you still have to report it as income and then remember that the same figure represents tax you have paid.

Then, there is the tax benefit rule about refunds and reimbursement. We have already looked at how that operates for medical insurance reimbursement. The refund of state income tax operates the same way, except that the figure that operates to limit income is the standard deduction.

Example: Cathy, who files as a single individual, had itemized deductions in 1996 of $4,300, of which $900 was state income tax. In 1997, she received a refund from her state for $500 of 1996 state income tax. She makes this computation:

Last year's total itemized deductions	$4,300
Deduct this year's refund	500
Itemized deductions if she had not overpaid her state income tax	$3,800

However, if she had only $3,800 of itemized deductions, she would have claimed the standard deduction of $4,000 instead. In other words, she received a tax benefit of only $300 ($4,300 minus $4,000). Therefore, she has to report as income just the amount of the benefit she received from the excess deduction, not the entire refund.

She does that by reporting the refund on the line for "taxable refunds" on Form 1040. Also, because the state reports the total amount of the refund to the IRS, she attaches to her tax return for 1997 a statement containing her computation.

If you made your last installment payment of state income tax for one year in January of the next year, that final payment is next year's deduction, not this year's. Suggestion: Make all state and local estimated tax payments no later than December 31 of the year to which they relate. That will make tax life a little easier and accelerate the deduction for the last estimated tax installment by one year.

If you use tax software, you need only input the amounts from your W-2 and the dates and amounts of refunds and estimated payments. The computer will sort this confusion out for you.

Foreign Income Taxes

These can be deducted along with state and local taxes, or you may claim a credit for foreign taxes you have paid. The foreign tax deduction or credit should be computed on Form 1116. The form and the eight pages of instructions can be overwhelming, but you may be able to ignore 95 percent of the instructions. If your only foreign tax is on a 1099-DIV from a mutual fund and is $200 or less ($400 or less on a joint return), there are short directions on page two of the instructions to Form 1116, headed "Exceptions to country-by-country reporting requirements." If you follow those directions, there is little problem in completing this form. Alternatively, if your foreign taxes are only $5 or $10, it is even less hassle to just claim a deduction on Schedule A.

If you have paid substantial foreign taxes, you may find it cost-effective to engage a tax professional to help you.

State, Local, and Foreign Real Property Taxes

This is fairly straightforward and simple. If you paid real estate taxes on real property you own, you can deduct the tax. That includes, of course, your residence(s).

However, there is a distinction to be made: Assessments for improvements (sewer line, sidewalk, and similar items that should raise the value of your property) are not deductible taxes. Rather, they can be used only as additions to the basis of the property, so the only tax break involved occurs when you sell the property. Notice that improvements *should* raise your property's value. It is not *necessary* that they raise it for the assessment to be nondeductible.

State and Local Personal Property Taxes

If the state or local government levies these taxes as taxes rather than licenses or some other fees, they are deductible in the year paid. The most common instances of these taxes are those levied on the value of vehicles and boats.

Interest Expense

Not all interest is deductible. What you can list as deductible are the following:

Home Mortgage Interest

Acquisition Debt

You can deduct interest on up to $1,000,000 of "acquisition debt," which is debt that is incurred in acquiring, constructing, or substantially improving your residence. Interest on debt incurred to refinance your original mortgage qualifies as acquisition debt, but only up to the balance of your original mortgage when you refinanced.

Home Equity Debt

You can deduct interest on debt that is not acquisition debt so long as it is secured by a mortgage on the residence and the total of both types of debt does not exceed the market value of the residence. There is also a total dollar limit of $100,000 on debt that is not acquisition debt.

Points

Points paid in connection with new acquisition debt are deductible in full in the year you pay them. Points paid for refinancing and home equity debt can be deducted ratably only over the life of the loan.

Investment Interest

Interest on debt that is incurred to purchase or hold investments, such as securities or a business in which you are passive, can be deducted. You cannot deduct more interest than you have investment income, but if that causes some of this interest to be nondeductible, that nondeductible amount can be carried over to future years and deducted when you have offsetting investment income.

Charitable Contributions

Your gift to a charity is an itemized deduction if certain conditions are met.

Is the Charity Qualified?

The organization must be operated for charitable, religious, educational, scientific, or literary purposes. Organizations for the prevention of cruelty to animals and those that conduct national or international amateur sports competitions also qualify.

If an organization solicits funds that are not eligible to be deducted as a charitable contribution, the organization must so state in every solicitation.

If you have a question about the status of an organization, you can check for the organization in IRS Publication 78. Many libraries have this sizable volume, and in it are listed most of the organizations that qualify as charitable organizations.

How Much Can You Contribute?

Of course, you can contribute all you want to a charity. However, your deduction on Schedule A is limited to a percentage of your adjusted gross income. For public charities, it is 50 percent. For private foundations, it's 30 percent. For some contributions of appreciated property it can be as low as 20 percent.

What's the difference between public and private charities? Mostly, it's the amount of public support of the charity, and the law defines a private foundation as any charity that is not a 50 percent charity. Rather than worry with involved definitions, suffice it to say that if you plan to donate more than 20 percent of your adjusted gross income, seek professional advice.

If you do contribute more than you can deduct, you have not completely lost the deduction. You can carry it forward and use it next year and the next year and so on, but you must use the deduction in five years or you lose it.

Be Sure You Can Prove You Made the Contribution

Sad to say, the folks at the IRS don't trust us. They want proof that we made a charitable contribution. Be sure you follow these rules and keep the record and documents for at least four years.

Cash Contributions of Up to $250

Your own records will suffice as proof of contributions at this level, and the easiest way to keep a record is to write a check for all contributions. The $250 is a test of each individual contribution, not an annual limit. However, do not write 52 weekly checks for $249.99 to the same charity. I doubt that the IRS would accept that procedure as complying with the rules.

Cash Contributions of $250 or More

The IRS says your canceled check is not enough documentation for these larger contributions. You must have a receipt from the charity, stating the amount of the contribution, as well as the name of the charity.

Gifts of Property Can Put Money in Your Pocket

You can give property instead of cash to a charity. More rules are involved, but they may be worth it if you don't need the property but do need a tax deduction.

Value of the Property You Contribute The value is the fair market value of the property, regardless of what it originally cost you. That well-worn suit you give to Goodwill is not worth $500. On the other hand, a contribution of that $1,000 worth of stock that cost you $50 years ago generates a $1,000 charitable deduction.

Income from Contribution of Appreciated Property When you donate securities or art that is worth more than you paid for it, and if you have owned it for more than 18 months so that long-term gain is involved, you pay no tax on that gain.

This is also true for contributions to private foundations if the contributions are made before June 30, 1998. (The 1997 tax code changes extended this deadline from the old one of May 31, 1997.) Contributions of appreciated property to public charities continue to escape the capital gain tax you would pay if you sold the property instead of contributing it.

Records and Documents You Need For gifts of property with a value of less than $250, your own record suffices. It should include a list of the property and the estimated value.

For a gift of property with a value of $250 to $500 you need a receipt from the charity. (With its usual love of "government-speak," the IRS describes the receipt you need as a "contemporaneous written acknowledgment."

For a gift of property with a value of $500 to $5,000, you need not only the receipt, but you have to complete Form 8283 and attach it to your return.

For a gift of property with a value over $5,000, you need an appraisal unless you are donating publicly traded securities. An appraisal summary (which is Part B of Form 8283) must be attached to your return. You keep the actual appraisal (in a safe place), unless the property is art appraised at $20,000 or more. In the latter case, include a copy of the appraisal in your tax return.

If you make a gift of art with an appraised value of $50,000 or more, you can request the IRS to issue a Statement of Value to you, which states what the IRS will accept as a value for your charitable contribution. It is not mandatory that you obtain this statement from the IRS, but if you don't like arguments and suspense, it's a safe course to take.

Ideas for Generating Deductions for Charitable Contributions

- Make a gift of appreciated property as already discussed
- Consider a Charitable Remainder Trust
- Think about a Charitable Bailout

Charitable Remainder Trust This allows you a charitable deduction for the cash or property you put into trust for your favorite charity, but you receive the trust income for life. Almost all colleges and large charities have a fund-raising department that will be delighted to help you set up the trust.

Charitable Bailout This works only for those who own a closely held corporation. If you fit that description, you can do this: Donate some of the stock of your corporation that you own to your favorite charity. Then, have your corporation use corporate cash to buy the stock back from the charity. *Voilà!* The charity has money; you have the charitable deduction; and you did not have to take additional (taxable) salary or dividends from the corporation. Of course, you have a little less of the stock in your mattress, but if you and your family are the only owners of the corporation's stock, that probably is of little consequence.

Casualty Losses

Casualty losses include losses from fire, storm, accident, and theft. For all but theft loss, there must be actual physical damage to the property, not just loss of value. Also, the loss must be from an event of a sudden, unexpected, or unusual nature such as a fire or storm. Deterioration over a period of time doesn't count. Theft includes larceny, robbery, and embezzlement.

Amount of Loss

The loss is the difference between the fair market value of the property before the casualty and the fair market value after the casualty. However, if the result of that computation is more than the basis (cost, usually) of the property, then the loss is the amount of the basis.

Example: Your house is damaged by a fire. From appraisals you ordered, it appears that the market value of your property before the fire was $150,000. The market value after the fire is $100,000, so the difference in fair market value before and after the casualty is $50,000. However, you purchased the house in 1970 for $20,000 and later added a room at a cost of $5,000, so your basis is only the total of cost of the house and the addition, or $25,000, and that, therefore, is the amount of your loss. (This example assumes you had no insurance.)

The amount of the loss is not what you deduct on schedule A, because the tax law says you can't deduct all the loss. Each casualty loss is reduced by $100, and then the total of all casualty losses is reduced by 10 percent of adjusted gross income (AGI, which is defined in Chapter 11).

Same example, enhanced: In the same year as the fire, your boat capsized and sank in a gale. That casualty loss was the difference in the before and after fair market value, which turned out to be $15,000. Also, your adjusted gross income for the year was $70,000. Now, your casualty loss for the year looks like this:

Casualty loss on house	$25,000	
Subtract	100	
Reduced casualty loss on house		$24,900
Casualty loss on boat	15,000	
Subtract	100	
Reduced casualty loss on boat		14,900
Total reduced casualty losses		39,800
Subtract 10% of AGI of $70,000		7,000
Deductible casualty loss		$32,800

That deduction probably translates into a reduction in your income tax of about $9,000, which is not much offset to losses totaling $65,000. Moral: Buy lots of insurance.

Insurance Proceeds

Insurance proceeds reduce the loss. In the above example, if insurance on the boat paid you $10,000, your casualty loss would be $5,000 before deducting the $100 and the 10 percent. If you choose not to file an insurance claim, the rules say you must still reduce your loss by the amount of the insurance proceeds you would have received if you did file a claim.

If the proceeds were for more than the loss, as they might be in the example of the loss on the house, you theoretically have a gain. However, if you replace the property with property that is "similar or related to it in service" within two years, there is no gain. Your basis in the replaced property is the same as it was in the damaged property.

Disaster Losses

If your principal residence was damaged by a disaster and your area was declared to be eligible for federal relief by the president, you have a choice as to when to claim the resulting casualty loss. You can claim it in the year of the loss or in the previous year, even if that means amending the return. For most people, claiming it in the previous year will hasten a resulting refund at a time when they need the money. However, you need to look at your tax situation in both years. You may be better off to take it in the year of the loss. For example, the previous year might be a low-income year, while the year of the loss might be high income when the casualty deduction would generate a larger refund or reduction of tax.

Theft Losses

The rules for deduction of theft losses are very similar to those for casualty losses. The one significant difference is that theft losses should be deducted in the year the loss is *discovered*.

Casualty, Theft, and Disaster Losses to Business Property

The rules for business property are similar to those for personal use property as described above. A significant difference is that if business property is a total loss, the loss is the basis of the property. The loss in fair market value is not significant unless the damage is partial.

How to Report Losses on Your Tax Return

All losses, both to personal-use property and business property, are computed on Form 4686. The totals from that form are carried:

- For personal-use property, to Schedule A.
- For business property, to Form 4797 if depreciable property is involved, or directly to Schedule D if depreciation is not involved.

Miscellaneous Itemized Deductions

This is another place where the government grabs more of your tax money. After you add up all these items that used to be fully deductible, you compute 2 percent of your adjusted gross income and deduct that from the total.

Example: Your adjusted gross income is $60,000 and you have $1,000 of supposedly deductible miscellaneous deductions. But you have to deduct 2 percent of $60,000 from your deductions, so you end up with $1,000 minus $1,200, or no deductions. (No, as of yet, you don't end up with a negative deduction on which to pay tax.)

There are many deductions that can fit into this miscellaneous category. The more common items are:

Unreimbursed Employee Expenses

These were discussed at some length in Chapters 3 and 4. Note that you cannot just plug in a total here. You have to get to this line on Schedule A by filling in Form 2106 first.

Tax Preparation Fees

You may be ahead to list these somewhere else than as an itemized deduction. For instance, if your tax return contains a business return (Schedule C), rental property (Schedule E), a farm (Schedule F), allocate some of the fees to these other schedules. The deductions on those schedules do not get reduced by 2 percent of adjusted gross income as do itemized deductions. Your tax preparer should allocate this deduction in the course of preparing your return without your prompting.

Other Expenses (Miscellaneous Deductions)

IRS instructions to this form tell you to list "amounts paid to produce income or collect taxable income and manage or protect property held for earning income." This makes it sound as if you list the expenses of running your business, your farm, your rental property, and your oil well here. That's not so. The business, farm, rental, and oil well expenses go on Schedules D, F, and E. The production-of-income expenses that belong under miscellaneous deductions are those that arise in your investing activities:

- Custodial fees (as for an IRA)
- Safe deposit box
- Investment counselors
- Costs of job seeking (including employment agency fees)
- Legal fees and court costs
- Legal fees involved in the collection of alimony and tax advice, but not other legal fees relative to divorce and separation
- Home office expense for investing activities are *not* deductible

Miscellaneous Deductions Not Subject to Reduction by 2 Percent of AGI

There are not many of these. The more common ones are:

- Impairment-related work expenses of a disabled person
- Gambling losses (only to extent of gambling winnings)

Fees related to other tax deductions are in this category, also:

- Appraisal fees for charitable contributions
- Appraisal fees for casualty losses

The Itemized Deductions Are Disappearing

Now that you have your itemized deductions computed and listed, they may disappear. If your adjusted gross income (in 1997) is more than $121,200 ($60,600 if you're married filing separately), the total of these deductions start to disappear, and they do that at the rate of 3 percent of however much your adjusted gross income exceeds $121,200 (or $60,600). When 80 percent of the total has disappeared, you get to keep the remaining 20 percent of your itemized deductions. (Isn't Congress generous?)

Conclusion

The heading says this chapter covered itemized deductions. Really, it covered how a timid Congress, encouraged by the IRS, and unwilling to tell us what it is really doing, has slowly raised effective tax rates. Slicing out parts of major deductions—7.5 percent of medical, 10 percent of casualty, and up to 80 percent of the whole—in effect, raises our taxes.

You'll find the next chapter just as exciting, for it tells you how all we have covered is put together in a Form 1040, the individual income tax return.

Winding Up—How It All Goes Together in Your Tax Form

WHO SHOULD READ THIS CHAPTER

- Everyone, for everyone who has to file an income tax return should have some idea of how it goes together

THIS CHAPTER INCLUDES

- How to take all the legal personal and dependents exemptions

- Find the best tax filing status

- How all the parts go together in your tax return

- Make the most of your losses

- Credits that reduce your losses

- The new scholarship credits explained

- How to keep out of trouble with the Nanny Tax

- Don't give away your Social Security taxes

- Don't be shot down by the Kiddie Tax

FAST FORWARD

Personal Exemptions and Your Tax Filing Status ➤ pp. 169–174

- Everyone knows about exemptions for yourself, spouse, and children. But there may be other relatives or friends who are eligible, and you might gain some deduction with a multiple-support agreement.

- Tax status is often simple, as when you are married and both of you work. But have your children grown? If you have a child who is married and a student, you have a direct interest in making sure he or she does not file a joint return.

- How all the tax information and calculation go together in a tax return is basic knowledge, but sometimes we forget an important part that could save tax dollars. A review doesn't hurt.

- Although net operating losses occur most often in corporation affairs, they do show up in individual income tax returns. They don't disappear, for they can be carried back, generating refunds, to prior years and the remainder carried forward to reduce future taxes.

Miscellaneous Tax Credits ➤ pp. 179–189

- Tax credits are the best tax attributes you can have, for they reduce taxes dollar-for-dollar. The new child credit and recent adoption credit offer some new opportunities for reducing the tax bite as long as you don't make too much money.

- If you become eligible for the Alternative Minimum Tax (AMT), you probably need professional help. But there are signs that tell you when the AMT might get you. That might be the case if you have high medical expense, funds from a home mortgage not used for your home, accelerated depreciation, incentive stock options, various intangible costs, pollution-control facilities, income or loss from passive activities, long-term contracts, installment sale income, foreign tax credit, investment interest, and net operating loss deductions.

If you have prepared your own tax return for years, the first part of this chapter may sound humdrum: filing status, dependents, and other details you deciphered years ago. Yet it pays to review even the basic rules now and then. Changes occur, and it's hard to keep up with all of them.

If you use a tax professional to prepare your returns, the same basic subjects may sound like something you leave to the professional. (Which deductions go on which line?) But professionals do make mistakes. They do misinterpret the information you give them, particularly when it all breaks loose in early April. It pays to have enough knowledge to enable you to review the professional's work. (Never, never, sign a prepared tax return and mail it to the IRS without studying it first.)

The last part of the chapter, which discusses credits that can reduce your taxes dollar-for-dollar, has some new information caused by the Taxpayer Relief Act of 1997. Specifically, in the area of education. Those credits will not be available until the 1998 tax year, but now is the time to start planning on how your family can use them.

Personal Exemptions

This is the part of the tax law where all the people you love get reduced to a few numbers. Each of them, if they pass through the maze of rules and tests that follows, can bring you a deduction of $2,650 (in 1997) of taxable income. Here are the rules:

- If you are single, you can claim a personal exemption for yourself. Exception: You cannot claim a personal exemption if you are claimed as a dependent on someone else's tax return. The usual occurrence of this is that your dependent child cannot claim the exemption because you are claiming him or her as a dependent.

- If you are married, you can claim a personal exemption for yourself and for your spouse on a joint return. On separate returns, each spouse claims his or her exemption. Exception: You cannot file a joint return and claim an exemption for a spouse if that spouse is a dependent of another. Example: A student claimed as a dependent by parents while married to an employed spouse.

Dependents Defined

To be your dependent, an individual must meet all these tests, which are summarized here and expanded upon later.

- Must be related to you or be a member of your household.
- The individual's gross income must be less than the exemption amount ($2,650 in 1997), but there are exceptions.
- You must provide more than half of the support of the individual unless there is a multiple-support agreement in place.
- The individual does not file a joint return unless the return is filed only for the purpose of claiming a refund of withheld taxes. That is, there would be no tax, before credit for any payments, shown on the return.
- The individual must be a U.S. citizen, or a resident of the United States, Canada, or Mexico.

Relationship Test Defined

The individual must be your child (including adopted), or a descendant of your child, a stepchild, your sibling (whole or half-blood), parent or ancestor of either, nephew or niece, brother or sister of either parent, or certain in-laws (brother-, sister-, mother-, son-, or daughter-in-law).

Member of Household Test Defined

An individual qualifies for this definition if he or she is a member of your household for the entire year. Note that individuals who are relatives do not need to meet this test, and individuals who meet this test do not have to be relatives.

Gross Income Test Defined

An individual with a gross income of more than the exemption amount cannot be your dependent unless he or she is your child who is under age 19 at the end of the year or, if a student, is under age 24. "Student" is defined as one who, during some part of each of five months of the year, is enrolled at an educational institution. (A full-time course of institutional on-farm training qualifies also.)

Support Test Defined

You must furnish more than one-half of a dependent's support, with two exceptions:

- If you are divorced or separated or have lived apart for the last six months of the year, you get the exemption if you are the custodial parent of a child. Exception to the exception: The custodial parent can release the exemption to the noncustodial parent. (Use Form 8332.) That either parent gets the exemption presupposes that between both of you, you provide more than half of the support for the child.

- The other exception arises when several people together contribute more than half of the support of an individual, but no one contributes more than half of the support. Those people can agree among themselves as to which one of them will claim the dependency exemption for the year. (Use Form 2120.)

Example: You and your two sisters, Betty and Barbara, each contributes 20 percent of the support of your mother. (The other 40 percent comes from Social Security benefits.) Neither Betty, Barbara, nor you can claim dependency exemptions for your mother, because none of you provides more than half of her support. However, Betty and Barbara can sign the multiple-support agreement (Form 2120), in which they agree not to claim a dependency exemption for your mother and they agree that you can claim it this year. (You could rotate this, so Betty gets the exemption deduction next year and Barbara the year after that.)

Your Tax Filing Status

Some people have the privilege of paying higher tax rates than do some other people. To find out if you're so lucky, you have to determine into which of the following categories you fit (your status is determined as of December 31):

Single Individuals

If you are single, you are one of those chosen to pay some high tax rates unless you can fall into one of the following other categories that pay income tax at a lower rate:

Qualifying Widow or Widower

To qualify, you must meet all these tests:

- Your spouse died in one of the two previous years. (To claim this status for 1997, your spouse must have died in 1995 or 1996.)
- You pay over half the cost of maintaining your home.
- Your home is also the home of your child, foster child, or stepchild, who is your dependent.
- You could have filed a joint return with your spouse for the year in which he or she died.
- You have not remarried as of the end of the year in question.

You cannot claim this status for the year your spouse died, but you can file a joint return for that year if:

- You did not remarry before the end of the year, or
- Your spouse died after the year ended.

The tax rates for this status are the same as those for "married, filing jointly."

Head of Household

As a single person, you fall into this status if one of the following circumstances is true:

1. You pay over half the cost of maintaining a home for a parent who is also your dependent. The parent's home can be a home separate from yours.

2. You pay over half the cost of maintaining your home, which is also the home for your child, grandchild, great-grandchild, or stepchild.
    *   If the child, etc. is unmarried, he or she does not need to be your dependent.
    *   If your child, etc. is married, he or she must be your dependent unless you are divorced or separated from the other parent of the child, etc. In that case, if the other parent claims the dependency exemption, the married child, etc. does not have to be your dependent.
3. You pay over half the cost of maintaining your home, which is also the home of your foster child or other relative not mentioned in (1) or (2) above. The foster child or other relative must also be your dependent.

In any event, you must be a U.S. citizen or resident alien for the entire year.

Happily Married Individuals

Married individuals have a choice. They can file one joint return or two separate returns. (If one spouse has no income, the other could file only a separate return, but it would be unusual for that to result in a lower tax.) When a married couple files separate returns, there is a special rate for the separate returns. The couple are not considered to be single except in specific situations when they are living apart.

Unfortunately, there are too many variables for there to be a rule of thumb as to the choice between filing separately or on a joint return. The only way to make an informed decision is to compute the total tax both ways and file by the method that results in the lowest tax.

Making a choice between separate and joint returns is generally the procedure if you are happily (most of the time) married, with exceptions.

*   If you or your spouse is claimed as a dependent on another individual's return, you may not file a joint return unless the only reason for filing a return is to claim a refund of all the tax that was withheld by employer(s). A common occurrence of a spouse being a dependent of someone else: The spouse is a full-time student and is being supported by his or her parents.
*   If your spouse is a nonresident alien, you may file jointly only if your spouse agrees to be taxed by the United States on worldwide income.

Unhappily Married Individuals

If your marriage has drifted onto rocky shoals and you have separated, these are the rules.

Joint and Separate Returns

Rules for married couples generally apply whether you are still cohabiting or have separated. Only a final decree of divorce or separate maintenance ends the married status. Before the final decree, the couple can still file a joint return if they can agree on it, or they can file "married, filing separate" returns. After the final decree, they fall into the *single* group covered above.

Head of Household

As usual, there is an exception to the rule: If you lived apart from your spouse for at least the last half of the year, and you meet the other tests described under "head of household" above (home for dependent, etc.), you can file as a head of household.

Joint Return Danger and Innocent Spouse

Before you sign a joint return with a disaffected spouse, remember that signing it makes you liable for *all* of any unpaid taxes, even if the tax liability only comes to light long after the return has been filed. That would be the case if the IRS audited the return and found that your spouse had not reported all of his or her income.

There is a concept called "innocent spouse" by which you might escape liability for the resulting taxes, but the IRS has a history of not accepting that plea, so attempting to escape tax liability by claiming you were an innocent spouse often requires a trip to federal court with its attendant legal costs and fees.

How It All Goes Together in Your Tax Return

Here are the steps that figure out how much you owe to your benevolent Uncle:

Step 1: Add Up Your Income from All Taxable Sources

- Wages
- Dividends and interest

- Alimony received
- Business and/or farm income or loss
- Capital gains and losses
- Other gains or losses
- Distributions from retirement plans and IRAs
- Income from rental operations
- Unemployment compensation
- Any other taxable income

Step 2: Compute How Much of Your Social Security Benefit Is Taxable

The resulting total is the number you need in order to determine if any or all of your Social Security benefits are taxable. (Obviously, you skip this if you are too young or able-bodied to be receiving money from the Social Security administration.) After you have made that determination (covered in Chapter 9), add the taxable Social Security benefits to the total you computed in Step 1. That results in a number that the IRS, quite logically, calls *total income*.

Step 3: Make Adjustments to That Total Income

- Subtract IRA contributions (provided they qualify as being deductible)
- Subtract deductible moving expenses
- Subtract one-half of the self-employment tax on income you earn in your sole proprietorship and/or partnerships
- Subtract deductible contributions you made to your retirement plan if you are self-employed or a member of a partnership
- Subtract any penalty you paid to a bank or similar institution for taking your money out of a CD or other savings instrument before it matured
- Subtract alimony you paid to ex-spouse(s)

Adjusted Gross Income

Adjusted gross income is the number you compute from steps 1, 2, and 3 above. You need this number in order to compute the limitations on itemized deductions, personal exemptions, and dependent care credit that are the next steps in the computation.

Step 4: Subtract Personal Exemptions

You can subtract only the net figures after computing any disallowed amount due to the phase-out rules for high incomes.

Step 5: Subtract Itemized Deductions

Again, you can subtract only the amount after computing any reduction for the 3/80 percent rule covered in Chapter 10.

Taxable Income

Taxable income is what is computed from steps 1 through 4. It is the figure on which you compute federal income tax, using either the tax table or tax schedule. (Be sure you use the correct table or schedule for your filing status determined earlier in this chapter.)

If your taxable income turns out to be a negative number, see the section on *net operating losses* later in this chapter.

Step 6: Deduct Nonrefundable Credits

The term "nonrefundable credits" refers to credits that can reduce your income tax to zero but not beyond. That is, it can never become negative. (A negative tax is, in effect, a refund paid directly out of the government coffers, not out of your tax bill.) Among these credits are:

- Child and dependent care credit (discussed below)
- Adoption credit (discussed below)
- Elderly or the disabled (discussed below)
- Foreign tax credit (covered in Chapter 10)

Tax After Application of Credits

This number can be zero but not a negative number. Even if taxable income is a negative, this is zero. (But see the section later on net operating losses.)

Step 7: Add Other Taxes

Notice that, by the way the math works here, you cannot use the nonrefundable credits to offset these other taxes. You have to pay these even if your income was a negative million dollars.

- Self-employment tax (Social Security tax on sole proprietors and active partners, as covered in Chapter 5)
- Alternative minimum tax (discussed later in this chapter)
- Social Security tax on income that used to get overlooked (as in *tips*)
- Taxes on retirement plans for withdrawals that are too early, too late, or other activities that are penalized
- Nanny Tax (discussed later in this chapter)

Step 8: Subtract Refundable Credits and Payments

- Earned income credit
- Income tax already paid by withholding, estimated payments, or payment with an extension request
- Excess Social Security tax payments

These last items can, and often do, develop a negative number, more commonly called a tax refund. Of course, if it's a positive number, you are supposed to write a check to the IRS for that amount.

Some of the above computation requires more explanation. That is what follows in the rest of this chapter.

Net Operating Loss (NOL)

It is possible to generate a negative taxable income. This can happen if you have large losses from a business (in which you are active) or a real estate venture (if you are active in a real estate business). In that event, you would be adding the *negative* numbers in Step 1, creating a negative adjusted gross income and negative taxable income.

If that happens, some of that negative income is a *net operating loss (NOL)*, and that can be carried back to the third previous year. By filing an amended return, you could apply that loss to reduce your income in that year, which would reduce your tax for that year and produce a refund for you. That's some compensation for your loss.

Notice that not all of a negative *taxable income* can be used in other years. Only that part that is *net operating loss (NOL)* can be so applied. To get from one to the other, start with the negative taxable income and add the deduction for personal deductions and some other nonbusiness deductions, such as capital losses, retirement plan contributions, and nonbusiness itemized deductions. (Where to find the details comes later.)

Example:

Laura's NOL in 1997 is $30,000. Her adjusted gross income for the prior years was:

1994	$ 20,000
1995	25,000

She would carry her loss back to 1994, wiping out the $20,000 income for that year, so she would receive a refund of all the income tax she paid for 1994. Because she would still have $10,000 of her loss, she would carry that to 1995, reducing her adjusted gross income to $15,000, which should generate a refund of part of the tax she paid for 1995.

If her loss was more than her income in 1994, 1995, and 1996, she does not lose the remaining loss. It stays in limbo until the end of 1998, when the remaining loss would be carried forward and deducted from her 1998 return.

The general rule is that NOLs can be carried back three years and forward 15 years. If you don't use it up in 15 years, you lose whatever remains. If your loss results from having to pay up for a faulty product you manufactured (product liability loss), you can carry the loss back 10 years and forward 15 years. Also, you can elect to forgo the carryback and carry only the loss forward, but you must elect to do that when you file the return of the loss year.

The calculations in determining the amount of a NOL are not as simple as they appear at first glance. When adjusted gross income is changed in a prior year, that affects other items, such as medical and casualty loss deductions. If there was a tax credit in the earlier year and, after the NOL carryback, the credit cannot be used, the credit can be carried back to even earlier years. If you were married in one of the years involved and single in another, or had different spouses in the years, there are more rules. In other words, it is an area that deserves professional help. (If you must do it yourself, order IRS Publication 536 and IRS Form 1045—that's where you will find all the adjustments—not just the most common listed here.)

Tax Credits in General

Some tax breaks are credits rather than deductions, and the distinction is important. A deduction generates a reduction in taxable income, so the reduction in tax is the amount of the deduction times your tax bracket. A credit is a dollar-for-dollar reduction of your tax.

Example:

Your taxable income is $50,000 and your income tax is $8,700. A $1,000 additional deduction would result in taxable income of $49,000 and income tax of $8,420, or $280 less tax. However, a credit of $1,000 would result in a tax of $7,700, which is $1,000 less tax.

Child and Dependent Care Credit

There are several hoops to jump through to get this credit. Those that affect most people are the following.

The Dependent(s) Must Be

- Under age 13 and a dependent. Exception: If, relative to a separation agreement or divorce, you have released the dependency exemption to your spouse or ex, the child need live in your house for only more than half of the year.
- Any dependent (or your spouse) of any age who is physically or mentally incapable of caring for himself or herself. For this test, the individual does not meet the gross income test of a dependent.
- Residing in your household, for which you foot more than half the bills for maintaining the household.

The Care Expenses Must Be Employment-related

- Both you and your spouse must be employed, or
- If one spouse is employed, the other can be a full-time student.

Amount of Credit

- The maximum is $2,400 for one qualifying dependent and $4,800 for two or more dependents, with the following limitations.

- The credit cannot exceed the earned income of the spouse with the lowest earned income. (For this purpose, full-time student status is the equivalent of $200 per month earned income if the care is for one dependent and $400 per month if for two dependents.) Earned income is wages, salaries, and self-employment in an active trade or business.

- The credit is 30 percent of dependent care if your adjusted gross income is $10,000 or less. It decreases at a rate of 1 percent for each $2,000 of adjusted gross income until it reaches 20 percent at $28,000 adjusted gross income.

- The credit is also reduced by the amount of assistance provided by your employer under the dependent care assistance nontaxable fringe benefit.

- Starting with tax returns for 1998, the credit will phase out for high-income individuals. The rules will be the same as for the child credit, discussed in the next section.

Expenses That Qualify

- Expenses for the care of the individual and household services qualify, so a housekeeper, maid, babysitter, and cook can qualify. However, payments to someone who is your dependent, your spouse, or your child under age 19 does not qualify.

- If the care is provided outside of your home, it is eligible for the credit only in the case of a child who is under age 13 or an older individual who spends at least eight hours a day in your home. If you send a dependent or spouse to a *dependent care center*, the operation must comply with all the rules of the state and local government if your expense is to be eligible for the credit.

  Be sure you have the Social Security number of individuals who provide care in your home and the taxpayer identification number of the operation that provides care outside of your home. (Exception: No taxpayer identification number is required from a tax-exempt organization.)

Child Credit

Tax credit for each child

Beginning with income tax returns for 1998, the law allows a tax credit for each child. (Sorry, you cannot take it on 1997 returns.) For 1998 the credit is $400 per child, and for 1999 and thereafter it is $500 per child. The amount stays at $500, regardless of any rise in the cost of living. It phases out for high-income individuals, based on adjusted gross income increased by any exclusion of income from foreign sources and from Guam, American Samoa, Northern Mariana Islands, and Puerto Rico. Those phaseout levels are:

- For married people filing a joint return $110,000
- For single or head of household taxpayers $75,000
- For married individuals filing separate returns $55,000

The phaseout is at the rate of $50 for each $1,000 of modified AGI.

In 2002, this credit will be reduced by one-half of the dependent care credit. There are some other limitations that are quite complex, involving FICA, SECA, and other adjustments to AGI. Describing them must await clarification from the IRS. The congressional conference committee that agreed on these complications more or less admitted it was beyond them. The report closed with the following:

> "The conferees anticipate that the Secretary of the Treasury will determine whether a simplified method of calculating the child credit, consistent with the formula described above, can be achieved."
> Good luck, IRS!

An eligible child is one under 17 who is your dependent and is your son, daughter, grandchild, stepson, stepdaughter, or an eligible foster child.

Adoption Expense Credit

Effective in the 1997 tax year, you can claim a tax credit of up to $5,000 for your expenses involved in adopting a child. (The limit is $6,000 for a child with special needs.) Expenses are eligible for the credit in the year after they are paid or incurred, except for the year the adoption is final and the following year, when they are eligible for the credit in the same year.

The credit is phased out if your adjusted gross income (AGI) is more than $75,000 and is gone when your AGI reaches $115,000. For purposes of this computation, your AGI is increased by the amount of any nontaxable income you have from a foreign country or U.S. possessions and Puerto Rico.

Eligible expenses are reasonable and necessary adoption fees, court costs, attorney's fees, and other expenses that are directly related to the legal adoption of an eligible child.

Credit for the Elderly or the Disabled

Who Is Eligible

To be able to deduct this credit from your tax, you must be age 65 or older or permanently and totally disabled. Also, a disabled individual must be receiving taxable disability income. If you lived with your spouse any time during the year, you must file a joint return.

Income Limits

If your adjusted gross income (AGI) is too high, you are ineligible for the credit. The amounts are:

	AGI Limit
Joint return, both 65 or more or disabled	$25,000
Joint return, one is 65 or more or disabled	$20,000
Single return	$17,500

Even if your AGI is less than these amounts, it is further reduced by the amount of Social Security or nontaxable veterans benefits you received. To find out if you can generate any credit, work out the numbers on the Schedule R that is attached to Form 1040.

Education Credits

For 1998 tax returns and beyond, there are two educational credits that you can deduct from your tax bill if you qualify. They are the HOPE Scholarship Credit and the Lifetime Learning Credits. One section of the tax law sets up both credits, so many of the rules apply to both, as follows:

*The HOPE Scholarship
Credit and the Lifetime
Learning Credit*

Phaseout of Credits

The credits are phased out for high incomes. Specifically, they start to reduce or phase out at modified AGI of $80,000 on a joint return and are down to nothing at $100,000 of modified AGI. (The phaseout level for other than joint returns is $40,000 to $50,000.) The levels will be adjusted for cost of living in 2001 and after. (Modified AGI is AGI plus excluded income from foreign sources, certain U.S. possessions and Puerto Rico.)

No credit is allowed for expenses for which any other tax rules allow a deduction (e.g., education that is deductible because it is work-related, as explained in Chapter 1). In addition, you cannot claim one of these credits if you have taken tax-free distributions from an education individual retirement account.

Either the HOPE Credit or the Lifetime Learning Credit, but not both, can be elected for each student for each year.

In other words, if you have two children in college, you have a choice between taking either credit or a tax-free IRA distribution for each. You could claim the HOPE credit for John and the tax-free education IRA distribution for Mary.

Eligible Student (for Either Credit)

You can take the credit for yourself, your spouse, or a dependent. If you are a dependent on someone else's return, you cannot use the credit yourself, but the individual who claims you as a dependent can subtract it from his or her tax. A married individual filing a separate return cannot claim the credit.

Eligible Expenses

These include tuition and fees at an eligible educational institution. They do not include tuition and fees for courses involving sports, games, or hobbies unless they are part of your degree program. Also not included are fees for meals, lodging, student activities, athletics, insurance, transportation, and similar personal, living, or family expenses.

Eligible Educational Institution

Generally, they are accredited post-secondary educational institutions offering credit toward a bachelor's degree, an associate's degree, or another recognized post-secondary credential. The institution must be eligible to participate in the Department of Education student aid programs.

Specifics of each credit are the following.

HOPE Scholarship Credit

This credit is 100 percent of eligible expenses up to $1,000 and 50 percent of the expenses over $1,000, up to a limit of $2,000 per year. That is, the maximum credit is $1,500. After 2001, those numbers will be increased for a cost-of-living adjustment. The credit is applicable to only the first two years of post-secondary education.

Lifetime Learning Credit

This is computed as 20 percent of tuition and fees incurred up to $5,000. (After December 31, 2002, the maximum base for the credit increases to $10,000.)

You can claim this credit for an unlimited number of years, and the study involved can be undergraduate, graduate, or professional degrees. Full-time and half-time study is covered, as well as less-than-half-time study to improve job skills.

Payments of tuition and fees made before July 1, 1998, do not count, so defer payment to that date if possible. Thereafter, you can pay tuition and fees late in one year for the next year's courses, as long as the courses start within three months of the second year. That will have the effect of accelerating some credit by one year.

Alternative Minimum Tax

Perhaps nothing is more of a manifestation of our convoluted tax system than the *alternative minimum tax (AMT)*. We have (through our elected representatives) installed complex deductions, credits, and nontaxable status of various income items in order to encourage wealthy people to make investments that we think will create jobs and grow a healthy economy. Then there are cries that the result is that the wealthy pay too little tax. What do we do? Undo what we have done? That would be too simple. Instead, we devise a separate tax system, the AMT, to reach those who take what we believe to be too many credits, deductions, and exemptions, even though the law allows them.

But the AMT affects not just the wealthy, for it can apply to anyone who takes various credits and deductions. The required procedure is that you compute your tax in the usual manner—as we have been discussing in this book. Then, following a separate set of rules, you compute your AMT. Then you pay the *higher* figure as your income tax.

If you have an uncomplicated economic life and moderate income, you probably will find that the AMT is well below your regular tax. However, don't rely on that rule of thumb. The only way to be sure is to check through the following list. If any of these apply to you, you should work out the numbers on IRS Form 6251 (you will need the IRS instructions also). To be practical about this complex tax, if only the first two items apply to you, you can probably work through the form by yourself. If any of the other items apply, it's probably time to hire professional help, or, as an alternative, use tax preparation software. Here's the list of what qualifies you to have to compute AMT:

- Itemized deductions for medical expense, taxes, and miscellaneous expense
- Interest on a home mortgage not used to buy, build, or substantially improve your home
- Accelerated depreciation
- Income from incentive stock options
- Tax-exempt interest from private activity bonds
- Intangible drilling, circulation, research, experimental, or mining exploration/development costs
- Amortization of pollution-control facilities
- Income or loss from tax-shelter farm activities or passive activities
- Percentage-of-completion income from long-term contracts
- Installment sale income
- Investment interest expense
- Foreign tax credit
- Net operating loss deduction

This is another area where your computer and tax software can save you a lot of computation and bewilderment, for it will fill in the Form 6251 for you. Otherwise, consider using a tax professional if the worksheet indicates you should fill in the form.

Nanny Tax (Domestic Service Employment Tax)

Even if you expect never to be nominated for a cabinet post and stand for approval before a senate committee, you should pay this tax. There are penalties, besides being unemployed, for not paying it. It's unfair to expect people to labor for you and not build up some credit toward Social Security retirement benefits. Look at the rates of tax (later in this section) and bear them in mind when you negotiate pay. (Remind the employee that he or she benefits from the Nanny Tax.)

Covered Employees

These include babysitters, nannies, health aides, maids, yard workers, chauffeurs, and similar jobs. To be considered employees, they should be subject to your control and direction (when to be at work and how to do the work). If you have these jobs done by a business that offers services to the general public, is responsible only to you for the results, and usually provides the tools, you do not have an employer-employee relationship—that is, you do not have to worry about the Nanny Tax.

If you do have an employer-employee relationship and any of the following are true, you will have to pay some Nanny Tax.

- You paid any household employee $1,000 or more during the year.
- You paid $1,000 or more to household employees in any quarter of the year even if no one employee was paid $1,000 or more.
- You withheld income tax from an employee's wages. (Withholding of income tax is not mandatory.)
- You paid any employee advance earned income credit. (If you do, you get your money back from the IRS.)

Rate of Tax

The FICA rate is 12.4 percent and the Medicare tax is 2.9 percent, for a total of 15.3 percent. In addition, you may also be eligible to pay state unemployment tax (the rate will vary with the state) and federal unemployment tax, which will be 0.8 percent *if* you paid your state unemployment tax on time. (If you failed to pay the state, the federal tax could be substantially higher.)

How to Stay Legal

As soon as it becomes apparent that you will be eligible to pay the Nanny Tax, call 1-800-TAX-FORM (1-800-829-3676) and ask the IRS to mail you Form SS-4. When you receive it, fill it in and return it promptly. (Unlike most IRS forms, you send no money with it.) The IRS will then notify you of the employer ID it has assigned to you, and they will put you on the mailing list to receive the forms and instructions you need.

As an alternative, find a neighborhood bookkeeping service to help you with the payroll forms. You do *not* need a CPA or similar tax professional for this job.

Excess Social Security Withheld

If you worked for more than one employer, you may have this situation. Specifically, if FICA was withheld on more wages that the FICA wage base ($65,400 in 1997), the total FICA withheld by both employers would be more than the maximum FICA you should pay. Note that this applies to the 6.2 percent FICA tax only, not to the 1.45 percent Medicare tax, so the maximum FICA tax you should pay in 1997 is $65,400 times 6.2 percent, or $4,054.80. If you paid more than that, claim the overpayment as a credit against your income taxes.

If you have only one employer and too much FICA was withheld, do not claim the overpayment as a tax credit. Instead, your employer should refund it to you.

Kiddie Tax

Time was when you could stack up investments in your young child's name and pay the child's lower rate of income tax, but Congress has put an end to that. The basic concept is that a child's unearned income pays tax as if that income were stacked on top of the parents' income. That is, it would be taxed at the parents' highest rate, or perhaps even higher. Notice that the tax applies to *unearned* income, so whatever the child earns from his or her own work is taxed as separate income of the child.

If Junior is your dependent, he cannot claim an exemption for himself on his return. However, he does get a standard deduction of $650 that is applicable to unearned income. The standard deduction is increased by the amount of any earned income up to the usual standard deduction limit ($4,150 in 1997).

For purposes of the Kiddie Tax, the rules allow a child to have unearned income of $1,300 (in 1997) before the Kiddie Tax kicks in.

Example: Mary, your 12-year-old daughter, is a wizard at programming computers, and earns $20,000 doing that on weekends. She also has a savings account that paid her $3,000 of interest during the year.

Mary's unearned income	$ 3,000
Subtract unearned income not subject to Kiddie Tax	1,300
Taxed at parent's highest tax rate	$ 1,700
Mary's total income	$23,000
Subtract income taxed at parents' tax rate	1,700
Subtotal	21,300
Subtract standard deduction	4,150
Mary's taxable income taxed as separate individual	$17,150

Although there are two different tax computations involved, both incomes and taxes are reported on the separate income tax return (Form 1040 or 1040A). The computations are made on Form 8615.

If your child has no earned income but only investment income, you can save a little paperwork by reporting the child's unearned income as your income. However, that is generally not recommended, for it increases your AGI, and that could mean fewer medical, casualty, and miscellaneous deductions to which a percentage of AGI is applied to reduce the deduction.

Child's Income Subject to Alternative Minimum Tax (AMT)

For 1997, a child's AMT is computed in the same manner as for all individuals, except that the exemption for AMT purposes is $1,300 plus the parents' unused exemption. This creates a need for some chaotic computations involving the parents' and the child's tax returns.

Believe it or not, Congress did take some action to simplify this process. Effective for 1998 and beyond, the child's AMT exemption is the child's earned income plus $5,000, and there is no longer any reference to the parents' unused exemption.

Conclusion

At this point, we have covered the hundreds of pages of tax law and regulations that tell us, as individuals, how to tax ourselves. Obviously, all the details, the minute regulations, and the various opinions of federal judges would not fit in this book. Rather, what I have tried to cover are the important points and some of traps you should avoid. What you should have by now is enough knowledge to know when you need help or when your tax software just won't handle your situation.

What follows in Chapter 12 is miscellaneous material you should have: guidance in choosing professional help and tax software.

Helpful Information

12

WHO SHOULD READ THIS CHAPTER

- Again, there is something here for everyone. Pick out what applies or interests you.

THIS CHAPTER INCLUDES

- More help from reference manuals that make sense

- How to save strain and grief with tax software

- How to pick the right tax professional for your needs

FAST FORWARD

Printed Help ➤ p. 193

- Choose a reference manual carefully. Some are little more than rewrites of IRS publications.

Software ➤ pp. 193–194

- Preparing your tax forms with the help of a computer can save a lot of grief and prevent errors. Pick a software program that will work on the equipment you have available.

Finding a Professional ➤ pp. 195–196

- Even if you prepare your own taxes, keep a professional on tap for advice and help in an emergency. Pick the right one for your situation.

More Printed Help

As I mentioned at the beginning of the book, there are thick volumes available that cover a myriad of details about our income tax rules. The sheer size of these books makes them an unlikely place to find a quick review of what could affect you. Now that you have found out where you stand in the tax picture, one of these hefty volumes can be a good reference, but do not try to read it page by page.

When you choose such a reference, beware of those that are little more than a rewrite of the free IRS publications. In fact, as I have pointed out often in this book, those IRS publications are a good first source of detailed rules if only because they are free. I suggest you order first those that cover the rules that affect you. If you find them incomprehensible, as many of them are, then run down to your bookstore and check out the volumes that are produced commercially.

Want a recommendation? My favorite is J. K. Lasser's 700-page volume, *Your Income Tax*. The book has been published annually for years, is thorough, well researched, and not just a rewrite of the IRS publications.

Tax Preparation Software

Do not be scared away from this subject by fear of the expense. Most software that will do an excellent job for most people is priced under $50. (Compare that to CPA rates!) If you do not have a computer, you probably have a friend who does.

As you are aware by now, I am a big fan of good income tax software. Given the present complexity of our tax system, I cannot understand why, or more important, how anyone could prepare a tax return with only a pencil and calculator.

How to Choose the Software You Need

First consideration, your computer (or the one you can borrow or, if need be, rent). You should determine the following about your computer:

- IBM compatible or Mac?

If IBM:

- What processor designation (286, 386, 486, or pentium)?
- How much random access memory (RAM)?
- How much space (in megabytes) is available on the hard drive?

- What level of DOS do you have?
- Do you have Windows, and if so, is it 3x or 95?

After obtaining that information, you need to assemble the important criteria for the software—you need to know what you want it to do. Specifically, now that you have read this far in this book, you should have a good concept of which tax areas that need to concern you. It helps if you can tie that down to the numbers of the forms and schedules you will need to fill out.

Also, think about how much help you need from the software. Some programs hold you tightly by the hand and lead you through a maze of "interview forms" that ask you many, many questions, most of which will not be applicable to you. Yet, if you have the patience, that type of program will cover every base for you. Other programs are form-oriented. You tell the program what forms you need, answer a few relevant questions the program will ask you as you come to each form, and plug in the numbers. Actually, there is still some hand-holding in this type of software, for if you need a schedule to support a number on a form, the software will lead you to the proper schedule.

Armed with the information on your computer's capability and your needs, you are ready to visit your software store and check the label on the tax preparation software. It should describe how much computer capability you need and tell you what forms the software will prepare. (You might have to open the box to find the list of forms. Just don't open the package that contains the disks, until you buy the software.) If it won't do what you need, look further. There is a program that will fill your needs.

If you don't like the crowds in the stores, or if you want a larger selection of software, here are telephone numbers of software producers. You can get the information you need over the phone.

Kiplinger Tax-Cut	800-235-4060
Personal Tax Edge	888-883-0791
Simply Tax	617-642-1700
Turbo Tax	800-446-8848
U.S. Tax	800-613-5157
A.M. Tax	800-859-8537

My favorite is A.M. Tax, because it will handle just about any possible tax situation, and inputting and processing are fast. Because their principal business is software for CPAs and other professionals, their personal program ($39) is form-oriented, with no time-consuming interview screens. Also, it will work on a machine as ancient as a 286. But if you want the hand-holding, call the other software suppliers.

Choosing a Tax Professional

Tax help comes in all varieties and sizes, from the individual who hangs out a shingle in the vacant store in January and leaves in May, to a partner in a Big Six accounting firm. To help you find the help you need and not pay for skills you don't need, here are some comments.

Commercial Tax Preparers

These range from the guy in the vacant store to the nationwide chains. Because there is no way to find out about the knowledge and ethics of the vacant-store operator, avoid him or her. The national chains usually do an adequate job for someone with wages, a mortgage, and perhaps a 401(k) plan. Although these companies have very knowledgeable tax professionals on their staff, they are usually supervising, training, or servicing their higher-income clients. If you just walk in, you take the luck of the draw as to the training and proficiency of your preparer. You are better off to call for an appointment with one of their knowledgeable people, but that is going to raise your costs to the level of other professionals who are licensed and regulated.

Enrolled Agent (EA)

Don't let the "agent" appellation scare you. These folk do not work for the IRS. They work for themselves or a private company, helping people like you contend with the IRS. You will usually find the designation of "EA" after their name, and they earn that designation by taking a lengthy IRS-administered exam. Beyond that, they are required to attend continuing education sessions every year, so they will be up to date on tax rules. Their enrolled agent status qualifies them to represent you before the IRS, so if you don't like handling an IRS audit in person, you can send your EA.

Certified Public Accountant (CPA)

The people with this designation also earn it by passing a comprehensive exam. However, this exam is administered by the American Institute of Certified Public Accountants (AICPA), rather than the IRS. In addition, they must hold at least a bachelor's degree with a concentration in accounting courses and must have worked in the accounting field for some time. The AICPA exam covers more than taxes, because CPAs are involved in many other areas besides individual taxes. Some specialize in auditing accounting records and financial statements, others are management consultants, and others concentrate on corporate taxes. For that reason, there is a caveat: Be sure that the CPA you engage to help you with your taxes does concentrate on tax matters. A CPA who is an auditor of accounting records may have some gaps in his tax knowledge.

Because they have a broad background in taxation, accounting, and management information systems, CPAs are usually the best choice if you operate a business that has outgrown the kitchen table.

Tax Attorneys

When you need one of these individuals, the key word is "tax." The ambulance chaser or the traffic court attorney probably knows next to nothing about federal tax laws. Fortunately, most nontax attorneys abhor tax work, so you are not likely to have an unqualified lawyer try to help you with your tax problem.

Although your CPA or your EA can represent you at the level of the IRS agent or the appeals office, you will need a tax attorney if your fight with the IRS leads you to tax court or another federal court. But a better use for a tax attorney is in the planning stages. If your CPA has a plan that can save you taxes and if the dollars involved are significant, bring a tax attorney into the picture. I suggest that course not because CPAs are incompetent (most are quite competent), but because two heads are better than one, and if the second head comes from another discipline (law), you are better off than having the two heads both belong to CPAs.

Conclusion

My goal was to not drop you at the end of this book and say "lotsa luck," but to leave you with some ideas on where to go from here. I hope I have succeeded.

Index